Mountaintop Boulevard
The Pilgrim's Journey Into Bliss

Gbenga Mathew Owotoki

Table of Contents

Dedication

To my Lord and Savior Jesus Christ. You are the reason why I live; you are the reason why I breathe. Thank you for making this possible.

To My Jewel of Inestimable Value, my best friend and dearly beloved wife, Eunice 'Rock Owotoki, thanks for your support, encouragement and prayers. You are the very best. Love you very much.

To my very own 'Pappi,' you have brought fullness to my life, love you loads, son.

Acknowledgment

A big God bless to all the leaders, officers and members of Hephzibah Network International Ministries for all the support over the years.

A special thanks to everyone that has played one role or the other in my journey so far. I appreciate you and say God bless you richly.

Preface

The journey to the Mountaintop Boulevard requires the utmost commitment and determination. This book highlights the life of Glory who is the major character in our story. His escape from Valleytown typifies a modern day reality for many believers today. This book is a must read as it is laced with deep truths and revelations from the Lord for the world, It is a message from the Lord to His Church. The life within Valleytown and what characterizes the various points within this town is revealed in this book. What does it take to escape from Valleytown? Is it really an easy path to the Mountaintop Boulevard? These and many more questions and answers are made bare in the book. It is a book that will be relevant many generations to come. I pray that the Lord will reveal Himself to you as you prayerfully with an open heart read through to the very last page of the book. You have a treasure in your hand. God bless.

Chapter 1

Life in Valleytown

Who could have believed that Pagan was the same child that almost died on the day of his birth alongside his mother? The day of his birth was a gloomy day for the family of Esuwamiri. Shortly after he was born, the mother bled to death; the local midwives watched helplessly, as they could do nothing to salvage the situation. Pagan almost followed suite as he developed complications shortly after his birth. The situations that surrounded Pagan's birth and how he survived left an indelible imprint on the father's heart; he dotted on him as a mother hen would do her chicks. Pagan was raised in abject poverty in a town called Valleytown. A town with very infertile soils and prolonged harvest seasons. Compared to other enclaves, Valleytown is reckoned as the poorest amongst the poor. The climate is unfavorable with extreme weather conditions; when the flood gate of heaven opens, it comes with so much rage that people scrabble for safety as the whole village becomes a river with floating houses and lifeless bodies of those who did not survive the torrent. And during the dry season, the sun with its blistering heat leaves the river dry and countless numbers of animal carcasses as a result of drought. The inhabitants are not left out as many, particularly the old, are unable to survive the blistering heat. The majority of the inhabitants are free thinkers who do not believe in the existence of the city called Mountaintop Boulevard not to talk of believing in its King. They are entrenched in the worship of a deity called Arogoto, who they believed is the ultimate protector of their town. Each year they offer sacrifices unto this deity to appease him. In Valleytown, man's inhumanity to man is the order of the day. The usual cliché of being 'your brother's keeper' is eclipsed by the wickedness that pervaded the horizon. People care less of what happens to the other. It is believed that the deity Arogoto has an unrestrained grip over the souls of those in this enclave by controlling their minds, dictating their pace and orchestrating their lives and desires. It is a Valley of doom and perdition in the real sense of the word. Fierce looking taskmasters called Sapagi, who have sworn allegiance to Arogoto, were given the mandate to watch over the land and ensure that the clan codes were religiously enforced and obeyed. Depending on the gravity of offense, citizens are either put in the prisons called holes, where they will not have access to food, water and even any form of human communications, or they will be killed outright in the most gruesome manner and in the open glare of the people in order to serve as a deterrent to others. Aside from these duties, the Sapagis' are known to forcefully take over other people's harvest and have carnal knowledge of the women, whether married or not, and nobody dares to question them. They are considered as the defacto gods of the land. Their words are law and their laws are harsh. With a careful look at the inhabitants of Valleytown, you would see shackles on the feet of everyone and children are not exempt. It is believed that these shackles restrict the movement of the people and as a result, they cannot escape from this den. This is a common feature of the land; ankles blackened by the grip of the chains. Escaping from this town is a Herculean task, as it is like passing through the eye of a needle. Only a very few have been able to escape successfully. Others who attempted using their own strength were captured and paid the ultimate price with their lives. Corpses of those killed were left in the open and it is not uncommon to find pieces of human bones and skeletons of those who attempted to escape in the open valley serving as caution to those who might want to attempt such a feat. Arogoto controls the minds of the people so it is rare for them to think of escaping from the gulag in which they have found themselves. Many had been brainwashed that the life they are living is the best they can ever have. Many had forever sealed their fate by completely selling their soul to Arogoto in exchange for power and fame. Such people are not difficult to recognize amongst the citizens, as they have completely different attire from the others. They are the 'go to' people and they enjoy special privileges that ordinary citizens do not. Regardless, they still have shackles around their ankles and are very unstable and volatile. Many of these people died early in life because of the covenant they made with Arogoto, and those who renege on this agreement are stripped of all they have acquired and made to die a shameless death. The enclave Valleytown derived its name because it was situated in the Valley with high crooked walls paved with sharp metals, making it difficult for anyone to climb or attempt an escape. Up above the wall is the command post where the Sapagis take turns watching over the town. There are two gates in the wall; there is a gigantic gate that is always left open and allows many people to walk into it daily but strangely, it does not allow people to exit.

The other gate is small, disheveled and can only allow for a single person to pass at a time. Close to this tiny gate are corpses of those who have been shot down in an attempt to escape. It is a petrifying sight to behold.

Although many have heard and been told of the beautiful city called the Mountaintop Boulevard, only few have succeeded in getting to the place. Many set sail but only few escaped from Valleytown and very few made it to Mountaintop Boulevard, even after the dare devil escape. The path is long, the road is tough and only the determined, those that have set their face as a flint, eventually make it there.

There also lived an old Sage in Valleytown called Wisdom. He lived in complete variance from the usual lifestyle found within the land. He was the oldest person in the town. It is said that Wisdom was never a citizen of the land but was sent as an Ambassador by the King of the Mountaintop Boulevard. Wisdom continued to live in the land regardless of all the futile attempts to eliminate Him. He was incarcerated many times, blackmailed and left in the dungeon for dead, but all efforts to get him silenced proved abortive. He was responsible for the escape of all those who succeeded in fleeing from Valleytown and was in constant battle with the Sapagis and Arogoto over the souls of the citizens of the land. It was believed that Wisdom was the supreme custodian of the treasure chest which included the treasure map to the Mountaintop Boulevard. Wisdom possessed the mastery and insight of the map, a map specially designed by the King of the Mountaintop Boulevard for the liberation of citizens of Valleytown and for direction on how they could journey through the Pilgrims Path to the Mountaintop Boulevard. This has been the instrument of escape for those who sought a better life on the Mountaintop Boulevard. This treasure chest has the powerful ability to change the lives of those who find it. Something strange about the chest is its endless depth. The more you dig, the more treasure you discover; it is endless. Arogoto and his buffoons know the intrinsic power of this treasure chest and have made every attempt to destroy it. However, they had always been met with staunch failure. Arogoto had come to the realization that the treasure chest was indestructible and he ensured that the citizens of Valleytown did not gain access to the treasure chest; he fought tooth and nail to distract the people so they would not pay attention to Wisdom. Gaining access to the treasure chest required contact with Wisdom, for He was the only one that knew where it was located. So you can imagine the security watch around Wisdom, and informants scattered all over the land who kept their ears to the ground for anyone who was attempting to dissent. If it were possible, they could have killed Wisdom, but it was not within their power as the old Sage had power over death. This was the world into which Pagan was born. A land of bondage and a place where you have to labor beyond the normal for you to earn the basic needs of life. A terrible place where you have to walk in shackles, thereby restricting your movement for the rest of your life. Wickedness and varying degrees of atrocities were common features in this land. Moral decadence was a daily lifestyle. Lanes and streets were named after the prevalent evil found in that space. They abhorred the King of the Mountaintop and did not hide their distaste for Wisdom. Such was the life Pagan grew up in.

Streets and lanes in Valleytown are well guarded by the gate keepers. There are restricted terrains and once people are in, they find it difficult to leave. Some of the streets and lanes found within Valleytown are:

Jezebel Street: Immorality and sexual pervasion are the lifestyle of those who live on this street. One in every two houses is a sex hub. Scantily cladded women are a common sight to behold. Adultery, fornication and all forms of sexual vices are the common occupations here; there are men killing each other because of women and women doing likewise. Within Jezebel Street, there can be found the sodomy threshold, a place where men are made to sleep with men and women with women. It is the high point of pervasion. A closer look at the inhabitants on this street reveals that they constantly live in fear and sadness because the street custodian regularly arrests the people and kill them to appease the god of the land.

Murder Jungle: When you walk into this street, you are greeted with a thick stench of blood. It is called "the land of brutality," where men are killed at will at the slightest provocation and most of the time there is no reason for murder; the people here derive pleasure from mowing and hacking others to death. It is not uncommon to see corpses and skeletons in the open field. People don't mourn their dead because it has become commonplace to see people dying daily in droves. Parents brutally killing their children and children equally doing the same. Spouses go for the jugulars of each other. It is a sorry sight. Their hearts are hardened. In addition, the custodian of this domain kills at will with the intent to appease the god of the land.

Deception trench: Every single person in this trench has stab scars on their back and it is common to see people walking around with a sharp object attached to their hands. Truth is alien in this terrain. Words spoken are not taken in their literal meaning; rather they have a different connotation. When they try to manage a smile, it means there is danger lurking around and when they say "good morning," it means "good night." People always look for ways to outsmart one another. They care less about who is hurt than about getting their way. Everyone is in possession of something that was not originally theirs.

Fool's Enclave: The entrance to this street has a bold inscription with the phrase, "Haters of the King." The occupants detest the King of the Mountaintop with a passion, and they never hide their disdain for Him. They believe in the nonexistence of the King and the Mountaintop Boulevard. Their words are always filled with profanity and curses, and passing derogatory remarks are a daily occurrence in this part of Valleytown. Every evening, large numbers of people from within and outside of Fool's Enclave gather to speak profanity against the King. The Fool's Enclave keeps expanding its boundaries to accommodate the ever increasing surge of people relocating to take up residency there.

Sorcerer's Coven: This Street is inhabited by those citizens who are completely sold out to the Chief god of the land. It is a common feature in this coven to see people practice stargazing, fortune telling, palm reading, necromancy, witchcraft and other forms of sorceries. People resolve to use these sorceries as a means of vengeance. Worthy of note is the fact that you don't need to offend people in this part of Valleytown for them to cast their spells on you. There is no daytime in Sorcerer's Coven; it is always dark and black as the night. Human and animal sacrifices are common features here.

These are the streets of Valleytown and there is a 'connecting alley' that links each street together as well as to the 'Illusion Trough,' which is the capital of Valleytown and located at the center. It is called "the land of falsehood" and the port of Authority. This is the melting pot for all people and activities within the city. All the characteristics for each streets are on full display at the centre and, even worse, it is the seat of Arogoto.

Chapter 2

The Escape

Pagan was raised single handedly by his father since his mother died during childbirth. His father dotted on him and tried as much as possible to shield him from the ravaging agents of Arogoto. Pagan grew up in Illusion Trough, also known as "the land of falsehood." While in his early teenage years, he became influenced by the lifestyle of one of the wicked kingpins in the land, who was named Rascal. Rascal was an oppressor and the fear he instilled in the land was enough to make the people have a breakdown. He was a loyal priest of Arogoto, who carried out inhumane treatment against others with much impunity. He killed at will and nobody could question him for action taken. He raped women in broad daylight and no citizen dared say a word or pass a derogatory comment against him. He is called "the terror of the land." In as much as Rascal was dreaded by most of the citizens, he was also held in high regard amongst the younger folks who saw him as their heroes. Therefore, they looked up to him for inspiration and guidance. Among this group of people was Pagan, who upon the onset of his teenage years became unabatedly wild. He was always found in the shrine of Rascal, alongside other young people, where they underwent indoctrination and daily brainwash. Pagan grew so wild that he left home and began to live within the corridors of the shrine. The father lost his grip over him. This was not unexpected, as the father was always under the influence of local liquor tapped from the tree and very common within the town. He was always drinking himself to stupor and wallowing in his vomit all night long. Even though he tried to offer Pagan some form of protection, he was also deficient because he was captured, beaten and incarcerated by the foot soldiers of Arogoto. Pagan's father had been the butt of all kinds of jabs; just name it and you will find him mentioned. He had been heard talking to him that he did not desire to live anymore and would take his own life if things continued to deteriorate. It was in the heat of all these things that Pagan picked up the habit of going to the shrine of Rascal and eventually turned into a street urchin. Not long after he left home, his father committed suicide. Before he killed himself, he left a note for him apologizing for his supposed failure as a father, stating how he loved him and had wanted to offer him protection, but he had to battle his own demons which eventually ruined his life. He left an instruction in the note that no matter what happened, Pagan should make an effort to find Wisdom, that He had the key to his freedom from this dark patch they had known as home. He said it would be a tough battle but if he is determined, he will come out victorious. He concluded by saying that Wisdom reached out to him several times but he did not give Him audience, and as a result, he had suffered terribly for this and would not want him to make the same mistake. He advised that Pagan should give Wisdom a chance with the hope that his life would change for the better. Pagan read this note carefully before any other reason could find it, but he did not pay much attention to it as he tore it into shreds and buried it.

After the demise of his father, Pagan made the Rascal shrine his primary home and sometimes he could be found sharing the open space at the Illusion Square with other urchins. Within a few years, Pagan had grown into a terrorizing figure in Valleytown. He is considered as a protégé of Rascal and an avowed soldier of Arogoto. Pagan was no stranger to barbaric acts; with a heart of steel, he had killed people at will, oppressed and violently usurped what belongs to others.

He became very influential and was made an honorary citizen of all the streets in Valleytown.

Due to his commitment and passion, Arogoto would always insist that he did his most awful assignments. Most times, he would be the one to go after the dissents. He had imprisoned quite a number of people who attempted to flee Valleytown and also oversaw their execution. He was also the coordinating chief in charge of sacrifices offered to Arogoto. Under his watch, a lot more people sold their souls to Arogoto.

At the time Pagan was in his early twenties, he had become a living terror, a complete opposite of that once innocent looking child who was given a second chance at life. He was always given to liquor just like his father and under that influence; a lot of atrocities were committed. He and his cohorts raped pregnant women and afterwards they ripped them open, took out the unborn children and offered them as sacrifices to Arogoto. At a point Pagan embarked on a trip into the evil forest entrenched deep within Valleytown in search of more powers. He was gone for weeks, dwelling in huts and shrines with serpents as his companions, and most of the time he stayed away from food. There were times when he stripped himself naked for days and allowed these serpents to crawl all over him. In his search for more powers, he met with a dwarf who was the high priest of the evil forest. He took him in and gave him an advanced tutelage in sorceries, laws and operations of Arogoto. He mixed several concoctions for him to drink and made special meals for him to eat. He placed an amulet around his waist and a necklace made from bids and ivory of an elephant around his neck. He made him swallow a live tortoise and gave him a strange sword for keeps.

The priest told him, "You are no more human since you have dined with gods and had been initiated into the inner caucus of Arogoto circles. You should be prepared for a higher responsibility because with all that has happened to you in this evil forest comes a greater responsibility. You are lucky to live through the experience because only a few out of the many that embarked on such trips eventually scaled through the horrendous experience and lived to tell their story." The high priest concluded.

Pagan left the forest a different person and felt he had acquired much more power to strengthen his stranglehold on the people and helped him scoop more favor from Arogoto.

The Assignment

Not long after the return of Pagan from his search for more power, he was summoned by the chief priest of Arogoto, who was the supreme ruler of Valleytown, for another seven days. He told him that Arogoto was well pleased with his devotion and was happy with his search and success for more power. He said with the power he has acquired, he is now ready for his next assignment. He told him that he had been chosen by Arogoto to curtail the influence and excesses of Wisdom among the people and to ensure that nobody had access to the treasure chest which contained the treasure map which would lead the people on the path to the Mountaintop Boulevard. He said that Arogoto was worried sick that he would be losing some of his ground to Wisdom, who was the able representative of the King of the Mountaintop, and that he had tried severally to curb this scourge but had always been met with failure. He had made attempts to kill Wisdom but it was an impossible task; he had attempted to search out the treasure map but each time they set fire on it to get it out of reach, the more it would glow, hence the reason why continuing to do that was a complete waste of time. As a result of all these failed efforts, the supreme ruler had resorted to the use of propaganda against Wisdom and the King of the Mountaintop Boulevard, as well as the use of intimidation against the citizens of Valleytown, of which many who tried to escape had been brutally murdered in the capital square to serve as deterrents to others who may be nursing such ambition. The chief priest went on to reveal to Pagan that Arogoto was once a citizen of the Mountaintop Boulevard and was one of the top officials there, but because of his breaking of the Mountaintop code of conduct, he was sent out alongside those that were in his support and, therefore, they pitched their tent in Valleytown. This experience led him to vow that he would make sure he prevents as many people as possible from finding their way to the Mountaintop. This had been his major goal. Although he had enjoyed a fair success rate, he was still not satisfied or happy about the few that had succeeded in escaping. He went further by saying that even after the citizen from Valleytown escaped from here, he still had controlling influence to a certain level to make them change their minds and cause them to return back to him; he had succeeded in doing this for so many years. He said that all through their journey from Valleytown to the gate of the Mountaintop Boulevard, it had always been a battle between himself and Wisdom for the souls of those that escaped. For some, he succeeded in bringing them back, and for others, he lost out to Wisdom and the King of the Mountaintop Boulevard. He said he was able to do this as a result of his dedicated agents that were working outside of Valleytown to distract and make the escapees lose focus and obscure their vision of the Mountaintop, making it look far away and completely out of reach. There are quite a number of routes and shortcuts created by Arogoto, which can make it easy for people on their way to the Mountaintop to return back to Valleytown, and such shortcuts come with their allurement and travelers find it difficult to resist this enticement; many had strayed out of the Mountaintop route as a result of this. He further inferred that the journey to the Mountaintop would not be a dash but a marathon, and there is no shortcut to getting there. It must be through the Pilgrims Path, which is a narrow, long and sometimes lonely path. Many grow weary and give up on the way, and it is the lifelong interest of Arogoto to ensure that they don't make it to the Mountaintop even after they might have escaped from Valleytown.

After the indoctrination, the chief priest of Arogoto inscribed the seal of Arogoto on the chest of Pagan and gave him a rod which he said should protect him from the overbearing influence of Wisdom, after which he commissioned Pagan to go and curb the influence of Wisdom and make it difficult for him to move around freely. Pagan was mandated to attack, incarcerate and kill whoever attempted to escape from Valleytown through the Gate of Decision. With these final words, and at the end of seven days, Pagan left the shrine of the chief priest.

The Confrontation

Pagan, alongside the others that had been commissioned for this task, put up surveillance to track Wisdom anytime He was on the move. They had spies and informants on every street within Valleytown who furnished them with information about those who they supposedly thought were planning an escape through the Gate of Decision.

Looking back a year later, Pagan and his team had recorded a fair success in their assignment. As it was anticipated, they incarcerated, killed and planted fear in the heart of the people so they would think twice before attempting to escape. But no matter how hard they tried to curb the influence and activity of Wisdom, they kept meeting a brick wall. In all of this, Wisdom kept having a growing impact on the people and had helped quite a number to successfully flee Valleytown.

The inability of Pagan and his cohorts to successfully curb Wisdom, coupled with the increasing number of those that fled the town, prompted Arogoto, through his chief priest, to summon a meeting. The chief priest was wroth and conveyed the displeasure of Arogoto. He said that although they had succeeded in preventing people from heeding to the appeal of Wisdom, a few more had escaped in the process, and this made things difficult for his agents on the Pilgrims Path as they needed to work overtime to entice them back. He said it was in their best interest to prevent them from getting out of Valleytown in the first place. After the chief priest had spoken, Pagan responded by saying that they had tried every trick that have been taught and even gone over and beyond in their strategy to ensure that they made it difficult for Wisdom to continue to convince and provide guidance and direction to the citizens of the land, but every one of their strategies failed. They found it difficult to hold Him down. The chief priest encouraged Pagan and his team and assured them of the rewards from Arogoto. He told them they would be staying at the shrine for an additional three days, where they would be further empowered to tackle Wisdom and curb His menace.

Upon departure from the chief priest's shrine, Pagan's immediate goal was to search out Wisdom and specifically confine His operations. "I am ready for Him." He said to himself, "Nothing can stop me this time." If only he knew what laid in wait for him, perhaps he would not have uttered that. Pagan called his men together and gave them instructions for what to do, after which he asked them to spread across the land with the sole aim of hunting Wisdom down.

Wisdom had always enjoyed His job of helping people discover who they really were by being their guide as they embarked on the very dangerous escape from Valleytown. Wisdom has piercing eyes which radiate love and compassion. Oftentimes, agents who had been given a mandate to make His access within the town difficult, ended up being won over by Him. Wisdom has a strong holding grip over people that come across Him. He is irresistible and at the same time, He would not force people against their will. He allows people to make the decision of whether they will go with Him or not. A contact with Wisdom is the beginning of liberation, which is why Arogoto will do anything to make sure He doesn't have free access to the people. He organizes events to distract them and increases their burden and pain, thus making it difficult for the people to think straight. He, through his agents, instigates war from within and without to disrupt the space in a bid to make it difficult for them to think of a possibility of escape, but in all of these, he never succeeded in slowing Wisdom down. He knows how powerful Wisdom is and what He is capable of doing. Wisdom is his nightmare and certainly a pain in his neck.

After a long day's job, Pagan had retired to his chambers in the wee hours of the morning. Not long after, he awoke to a rattling within his room. He went back to see if he had properly locked the door and, true to his assumption, the door was properly locked. As he turned to return back to lie down, he saw Wisdom sitting at the edge of his bed. He quickly reached out to the amulet he had around his waist and recited some incantations, after which he lifted up his hands to strike Wisdom but Wisdom, looking unperturbed, just laughed mildly. Pagan became still and could not move even though he was still alert. Wisdom, with a gentle smile said to Pagan, "Why have you sold your soul to Arogoto?" He told him that he had appeared to him several times in his dreams to point him to the path of freedom but knew that his heart has been seared with hot iron. He said that the assignment from Arogoto could only quicken his journey to destruction, giving examples of those that had been given similar assignments. He laid hands on Pagan and felt, as it were, an electric sensation which flowed through his body. He felt something move out of him and he felt light. The presence of Wisdom was overwhelming. Pagan could not fathom what was happening. His mind began to open up. Before long, he began to sob. Wisdom further laid hands on his eyes and it was as if scales fell off his eyes and he saw for the first time the shackles around his legs and immediately Wisdom pointed at the shackles; they were broken. Whilst this happened, Pagan remembered the last words of his father on how he advised him to give Wisdom a chance, as He holds the key to his liberation. At this point, everything began to make sense to him. Wisdom went ahead to reveal that the ultimate goal of Arogoto is to eventually destroy all the citizens of Valleytown, including those that have diligently served him. Wisdom reached out for his white garb and took out the treasure chest he brought with him. He began to instruct Pagan on the significance of its content. He talked about the protective armor as a very important defensive and offensive weapon for his journey. He also handed him the operative manual for this armor and, being soon to commence the journey, instructions for how to operate it and what to do when any part of the armor is defective. He handed him the treasure map which contained the route and instructions on how to navigate to the Mountaintop Boulevard. He told him that the journey will be long and tough but His ever abiding presence will be with him. He said escaping from Valleytown is just the first step in his journey.

"There will be distractions as you travel along and sometimes it will seem you are the only one traveling on the Pilgrims Path, but be encouraged because many have been called out but only few will go through it to the very end." He said. Wisdom further admonished Pagan that his heart must be made up for the journey because Arogoto will do everything to get him back. Pagan, after listening to all that Wisdom had to say, was so full of joy that he told Wisdom of his decision to leave Valleytown and damn the consequence. He said that he had never felt such peace as he felt now, and he could see that he had been grossly brainwashed and blindfolded to do the selfish biddings of Arogoto. Wisdom further laid hands on him, strengthening him for the journey. He also told him that he will meet with fellow travelers as he journeyed and he should be careful because some of them might have been compromised for some unwholesome reasons and they would want to sway him from the Pilgrims Path, which is the only path that leads to the Mountaintop Boulevard. He said that whenever he is faced with such a situation or when confused, he should search the manual and treasure map and follow the instructions there. Whilst this happened, the chief priest of Arogoto suddenly woke up from sleep and saw that one of Arogoto's effigies had fallen face down; he immediately knew something was amiss. He looked through his crystal ball and saw that Pagan had been stripped of his powers but could not figure out exactly how it happened. He immediately called for a meeting with all the other foot soldiers of Arogoto and together they went in search of Pagan. When they got to the place he was, Pagan stepped out of the house and what they saw bemused them, as the person standing before them was a completely different person. His gregarious personage was no more. All the amulets, necklaces and chains were no more. The chief priest could see that all he had swallowed during his initiations were gone. Distraught, he asked, "What happened to you?" Pagan replied, "I have seen the light and I no longer belong to

Arogoto. I am now a potential candidate of the Mountaintop Boulevard." He said this with a tone of finality. Immediately, the chief priest and the rest of his smug followers heard that; they were confused and were in complete disarray. The chief priest screamed at Pagan with utmost vulgarity, telling him he has eating the forbidden fruit and will certainly pay the ultimate price for this. He asked the agents with him to seize him and put him in chains but, as they charged towards him, Wisdom came out and immediately there was a force that repelled them. They made another effort, but they could not come close to Wisdom and Pagan. When the chief priest saw their effort was futile, he resorted to appeals and blackmail. He told Pagan that he was making the costliest mistake of his life, that neither Wisdom nor the King of the Mountaintop had anything to offer him. He told him to think about the power he was giving up by leaving Valleytown and the promises made to him by Arogoto. He told him to look at the people around him who looked up to him for inspiration. He said that he must be foolish to let go of all of these. He pleaded passionately with him, and all the other agents that had now joined in the confrontation wept and tried to sway him. Pagan put his hands in his ears and, with tears in his eyes, shouted at the top of his voice that his mind was made up and there would be no rescinding on his decision to follow Wisdom. They made another final push to attack him but they could not come near him because of the presence of Wisdom, who did not utter a word during this whole confrontation. The chief priest, at this point with his eyes as red as scarlet, belched and spoke sternly to Pagan that he will never make it through the Gate of Freedom, that they will be waiting for him there to make sure he does not go through the gate. After saying these things, they all left. Immediately, there was a message sent to the keeper of the gate telling him to be alert, and re-enforcement was sent to fortify the gate and a round-the-clock surveillance was issued. They were prepared for battle as they considered the anticipated escape of Pagan, an escape too much to bear.

Wisdom looked into the eyes of Pagan and, with His hands on his shoulder, affirmed that he was proud of his decision to flee from Valleytown. He said that decision is not enough, he needed to act and take the bold step to leave this hole and He assured him, He will make his escape easy but he must be the one to take the step to leave. He must do it now because Arogoto would not be happy he had lost him and would do anything to prevent him from going through the Gate of Freedom. Wisdom further said, "For you to escape from this valley without glitch, you need to walk with me." He said that when he walks with Him, they will not see him but Him. He told him that that is the secret of freedom with ease, and that many people who were captured and killed in the process of their escape failed to abide by this instruction, but the few who did, escaped from Valleytown successfully. He said that even Arogoto does not know about this secret and he cannot attack nor fight what he does not know.

Pagan, having heard all that was said by Wisdom, asked how it was possible to walk with him, to which Wisdom responded that it is a mystery; all that is required is for him to make that decision and to be determined. Pagan thereafter told Wisdom that he was willing to walk with him. Wisdom responded that based on his confession and willingness, He will lead him through the Gate of Freedom right away. Meanwhile, the chief priest of Arogoto had sent words out to all the foot soldiers to be on the lookout for Pagan and had fortified the Gates of Freedom. He also sent in some of his fiercest soldiers to keep watch over the gate.

After their conversation, Wisdom took Pagan by the hand and led him through the heavily secured Illusion Square to the path that leads unto the Freedom Gate. Nobody stopped Him, and neither could anyone harass Him. When he got to the gate, the security search light beamed on Him but no one dared prevent Him. The gate opened of its own accord without any effort from Him, and Wisdom thus took Pagan through the Gate of Freedom.

A Breath of Fresh Air

Immediately, Pagan crossed the gate. He felt extremely light and there was this quietness that came from within, such that could not be described. The tanned armor he was wearing automatically came off him and he was completely transformed, as he was clothed with a completely new set of armor different from what the foot soldiers of Arogoto were used to putting on. There was this cool mien around him. Pagan, who was once a dreaded terror in Valleytown, had grown to become as gentle as a dove. Pagan asked Wisdom, out of curiosity, that he was surprised that despite all the threats by Arogoto and his buffoons, none of them had put up a fight during the time of his escape. Wisdom gave a hearty laugh and, fixing His eyes on Pagan, told him that all through that period he (Pagan) was invincible to everyone looking to stop him from escaping. Wisdom said, "That is the secret of walking with me. All those who choose to completely walk with me become invincible to the enemies. They are not seen. They will have to deal with me to get to them. Arogoto is limited in his operations and power and whosoever stays with me in this journey will be able to navigate through the traps and murky road bumps set by the enemy." Whilst Wisdom was speaking, Pagan saw multitudes running into Valleytown through the broad gate; he beckoned and tried to stop them but no one listened to him. He turned to Wisdom and asked, "Why are these people running back into Valleytown?" Wisdom responded, "These are people who had similarly escaped from Valleytown at some point but had given up on their pursuit to get to Mountaintop. Some were lured back with the deception of a better life when they returned, others got weary because they felt the journey was excruciatingly long and, when they thought they were getting close, it seemed that the journey got farther for them. Others sought a shortcut without going through the proper route as indicated on the treasure map, and when they thought they were heading to the Mountaintop, they found themselves on a detour leading back to Valleytown. For some, they simply became so full of themselves that they ignored the instruction in the manual given to them, as they believed that they could complete the journey through their own path. For others, they were just simply careless and, before they could get up from their slumber, they found themselves back in Valleytown. Some of these people returning back will rediscover themselves and return to make the journey again, but they would have lost some ground in the process."

Wisdom further told Pagan, "Henceforth, you will be called by a new name as your escape has transformed you into a new being. Everyone that fled Valleytown is given a new name to symbolize their new lease of life. You will now be called Glory. You have been given this name because there is a greater glory that awaits you at the end of this journey. Your escape from Valleytown is just the first step in getting to the Mountaintop. At no point should you feel self sufficient and thus decide you do not need me in this journey. You must diligently study the manual and obey every instruction contained therein. There is no shortcut to the Mountaintop. Don't allow anyone to deceive you. The only path remains the old rugged Pilgrims Path. You must be careful of people and agents of Arogoto who will come in fake armors similar to what you have on with the intent to present you with another path. Whatever is not in agreement with what is written in the manual should be avoided." He warned.

While Wisdom spoke with Glory, he heard several distinct, amplified voices of people (of which he was later told by Wisdom were voices of some of those who had escaped from Valleytown) calling on the citizens of Valleytown to flee from the land because of the impending danger that will befall the town. The voices were so loud that he was surprised why he could not have heard this while he was within Valleytown because there was no way people couldn't have heard. Wisdom, seeing the curiosity of Glory, said, "There are few people within the town that can hear these distinct voices, but Arogoto has made the people to be dull of hearing as they could not comprehend the meaning of what was said. And for the majority, it was difficult for them to hear because of the noise created by the stooges of Arogoto who had been assigned to distract the people, hence making it difficult for anyone to have heard such warnings." He admonished Glory on the need to be one of the voices that will warn the people within from outside the Freedom Gate.

After Wisdom shared this very vital instruction with Glory, He said it was time to continue on His journey, and He pointed a path through which Glory must travel.

Chapter 3

The Discovery Avenue

Glory turned from Wisdom with the assurance that Wisdom will always be with him whenever he calls on Him. Glory walked in the direction he was pointed, and at the entrance was an isolated rock with the inscription, "The Discovery Avenue - A place where you discover the Who, the Why, the What, the When and the Where." As Glory pondered on these, a man walked up to him, clad in the same armor but with some dents on his and the sword he had was stained with blood, and he introduced himself as Mentor. He said to Glory, "There are several of us who the King of the Mountaintop Boulevard has positioned to help those who are just embarking on the journey through the Pilgrim's Path. Some pilgrims, after their escape from Valleytown, decide they do not need his guidance as they travel through the Discovery Avenue, and quite a number eventually end up falling prey to the schemes of Arogoto as well as his agents. I am here to make your trip easy and to help you discover yourself, but it is a matter of choice for you." Glory remembered the words of Wisdom, to always check from the manual and from Him whenever he was confused, and in the quietness of his heart he called to Wisdom and asked if it was right to go with Mentor. Wisdom showed up and was glad that he could call on Him. He said, "Mentor is one of those who have gone ahead in this journey and has fought several battles as he has travelled through the Pilgrims Path. He won most of his battles and lost a few, hence the dent you see on his armor. He has gone through the Discovery Avenue and has become one of the people placed on this path by the King to help those coming behind. He has been instructed to share his many triumphs and his mistakes with you as a way to encourage and admonish you, but never cease to cross check from the manual. As this is the ultimate guide, anything you are told that is not backed up by the manual must be rejected. But I must say, it is your call to either go with him or not." He concluded.

After thinking for a while, Glory called unto Mentor and told him that he would be pleased to have him lead him through the Discovery Avenue, and thus the journey of Glory through the Discovery Avenue began.

Who Lane

Fully kitted in his armor, Glory went in together with Mentor (who was already familiar with the terrain) through the first gate called the "Who Lane." Mentor assured Glory he was there to guide him, but he should always check with Wisdom because He is the ultimate guide. The journey through the Who Lane was an eye opener for Glory. He was shocked to see his old lifestyle played out right in front of him. His ruthlessness and inordinate quest for power and relevance, his loyalty to Arogoto and even his young teenage years were all captured and played back right in front of him. He asked Mentor, "Why do I have my whole life playing before me?" Mentor responded, "Everything done in Valleytown, and even on this trip through the Pilgrims Path, is recorded and no one will have any excuse, not even Arogoto, to deny all that they have done. After escaping from the land of falsehood, every record of all the wickedness you had done was removed from the active folder to the inactive one. All that you are seeing is to make you appreciate the transformation that has occurred in your life. This is the first step in realizing your true identity. A review of your past is meant to make you realize that is not who you truly are."

Mentor continued, as he had his eyes fixed on Glory, "After the escape from Valleytown, the process of realization is not instant; it is a process in time and this journey through the Discovery Avenue is meant to bring you to that point of realization." At this point, Glory asked Mentor, "Who am I?" Mentor replied, "I am glad you have asked this question because everyone who is serious about his journey on the Pilgrims Path must definitely ask this question. Since you have realized who you are not, discovering yourself involves an in-depth study of the manual you were given by Wisdom and, oftentimes, my guidance can help shed light on the grey areas of your life." When Mentor was done talking, the image of Glory's past was lifted from him and what he saw next marveled him; he saw a bright light flash before him and he heard one of the sweetest voices ever saying to him, "You are the son of the King, that is who you are and you have been bought with a price. Arogoto knew this and fought tireless to make sure you did not discover this truth. That was why he held you bound to himself and utilized your strength for his own selfish interest. For you and the others to be rescued, the King had to mandate Wisdom to complete the process of liberation, which was started by Prince Charming, the only Son of King Ultimate, the Supreme ruler of

Mountaintop Boulevard." A smile lit up on Glory's face and with an air of relief, he jumped with excitement, reminiscing on his liberation from the dungeon called Valleytown. "You have been set free for a purpose. Everyone born into Valleytown has a purpose to fulfill, but Arogoto had worked to ensure that nobody fulfilled his or her original purpose. What he did was to swap their destiny in exchange for regrets and confusion. Many were meant to be life savers and solution providers, but Arogoto took all that away and they became the problems that required solution and the people who really needed help with their lives. Many great reformers and transformers had been made captive and, as a result, their purpose in destiny thwarted. Some are also living in a false realization of what their purpose is. Arogoto thrives in an atmosphere of confusion. He derives pleasure from seeing people living a false life and he will stop at nothing to ensure that people don't truly discover who they are. Do not forget that Arogoto still had strong influence even as the liberated journey through the Pilgrims Path. That is why many of those who fled Valleytown eventually returned back to that gulag and only a few made it through to the Mountaintop Boulevard," the voice concluded. After these words, Glory came to a full realization of who he was.

Mentor further helped him to understand that what he has learnt was a fundamental key to his successful journey through the Pilgrims Path. He said, "There are pilgrims whom I had come across who were either not patient enough to discover who they were or were never truly concerned to discover themselves. Such people, whenever they were faced with difficult times, eventually fell prey to these unpleasant circumstances. Although some may recover along the way, they would have lost some precious time, and some were not as lucky, as they became easy targets to the jabs of Arogoto and his cohorts who are always ready to strike at very vulnerable moments during this journey."

After all that happened in the Who Lane, Glory was led into the "Why Lane" as he walked closely behind Mentor.

Why Lane

Walking through the "Who Lane," there was a short corridor with a gate that led into another section of the Discovery Avenue. On the gate was an inscription, "Why Lane." Mentor mentioned to Glory about how important the Why Lane is. He said, "This is the place where the purpose of every pilgrim is revealed. Knowing who you are without understanding why you are here or why you have been framed the way you are will make the journey a difficult one. Every pilgrim has been liberated to make a difference as they journey through this path en route to the Mountaintop. For example, Prince Charming's purpose for stepping down to come into Valleytown was to pay the price for the freedom of everyone in that town and, even though the price had been paid, it is still imperative that the people accept this gesture by taking a personal step to be freed. That was His purpose and He lived it to the fullest. The King of the Mountaintop by whom everything was made, gave special gifts and abilities to everyone, and Arogoto recognized this and blinded the eyes of the people to this reality such that even if they will put their gifts and talents to use, they will be used for his own gain and for his personal aggrandizement. Many of his foot soldiers had been given great abilities which were meant to be channeled for positive use and influence, but he blinded their eyes to these realities so he made use of them for his gain. Many people will never realize this truth because they will not be alive to discover it." Looking at Glory, he said to him, "You are fortunate in that you have been able to discover these truths. You were able to do all you did for

Arogoto because he saw the great abilities you have been blessed with, and he took advantage of you for his own selfish reason, using you to carry out his nefarious activities of carnage and awful pogrom. You are greatly blessed. Many of your colleagues were not as fortunate and many more will never be. A walk through the "Why Lane" is to make you understand the reason why you were born and also why you have been liberated, and you will need to discover the purpose for both. To understand the reason for your birth, you will need my guidance because I have been on this journey for a while and understand the terrain better. I have fought battles and won many victories, so that is why I have these dents on my armor. I have encountered a lot of people on this path and I can tell you there is nothing new on this path. My meeting with you and spending this moment with you on this Discovery Avenue gives me an insight into the purpose for your life and, trust me, I am well equipped for these tasks." Glory listened with rapt attention while Mentor continued, "The second path of discovery is found in the reason why you have been liberated and for you to discover this, you will need to consult the manual given to you by Wisdom. This is the ultimate source of finding out the purpose for your liberation from the grip of Arogoto. This purpose differs with individuals but there is a common denominator for everyone, and that is to ultimately do the will of the King and eventually make it through to the Mountaintop." Mentor further admonished the need to constantly consult with Wisdom as He inspired the writing of the manual. He said, "Some information within the manual may not be of express interpretation, hence the need to constantly be open to Wisdom for insight. Regardless of the number of battles I have fought and won, I draw great strength and comfort from the manual. A pilgrim begins to diminish and becomes vulnerable when his dependency on the manual begins to wane. Understanding the 'why you are here' cannot be done independent of Wisdom. The degree of dependency on Him will determine the degree of our impact and manifestation as we journey through, and this you will experience as you continue on the Pilgrims Path." Mentor made Glory to realize what he has shared with him was what had made the difference in the lives of some Pilgrims. "Not everyone will understand all I have made known to you, and some will not even understand after traveling through the Discovery Avenue, but blessed are those who go through this and live out what they have been taught." Mentor concluded. Glory, who had listened with rapt attention, responded, "I am beginning to appreciate how important it is to have come through the Discovery Avenue. I know this will help me to be better equipped for my journey. I have been able to discover what my true identity is and now, through your help, I have been able to realize why I was born in the first place and the purpose for which I was liberated from Valleytown. I now understand that the grand enemy Arogoto discovers the purpose of the people within his grip and uses this to his advantage, and that was why he got me involved in leading onslaughts and made me a captain amongst his soldiers, because he knew I was born to lead and he saw this potential and utilized it to the fullest. I wish I had realized this a long time ago. Now my eyes are open and I have made up my mind to channel this ability in a positive way to help others that I come across, just as you (Mentor) have helped me. I know one day I will be able to help others, too, on this Pilgrims Path." Glory said. Mentor, beaming with smile, said, "I am glad you have been able to discover who you truly are and why you are here. When you have the right sense of purpose, every other thing falls into place and, above all, you have been able to realize that the ultimate reason why you have been rescued is to make it to the Mountaintop. Besides, this is also the underlying reason of service to others and to the King. What I am doing now is part of my service connected to my purpose. Everyone has a path cut out for him; what is important is discovering this and walking in that path." Mentor took Glory by the hand and they advanced to the next lane.

Where Lane

They came through a lane with the bold inscription "The Where Lane," and the first thing that struck Glory is that there were several sections with each having their own path. Mentor made him realize that a lot of people had made grave mistakes because they did not know where they were heading, and when you do not have an understanding of where you are going, any route will lead there but unfortunately, the 'there' they eventually end up at might become their Waterloo, hence the need to be very careful. Wisdom reiterated again that the ultimate destination for every pilgrim is to make it to the Mountaintop, but there are destinations peculiar to individual pilgrims that have been locked into their journey through this path. He said, "It is the desire of the King for his children to live fulfilled lives and to be blessed. He said that our fulfillment is found in the individual destinations called Pletholand. It is a place of abundance which should reflect in every facet of a pilgrim's life and because our destination is connected to our purpose and who we are, we will not miss it for anything when we get there. Some people have taken the wrong path within the "Where Lane" and have missed their Pletholand. It is important to understand that there is a correlation between individual Pletholand and their making it to the Mountaintop. A man who takes the wrong path will eventually find himself in the wrong Pletholand; hence, it's very important to know why you are here." He further said to Glory, "There are a lot of people who could not make it to the Mountaintop because they could not locate their Pletholand. You should know that Arogoto is still very much interested in ensuring that those who have escaped are recaptured and brought back to his enclave. One of the many ways he employed was to ensure that pilgrims are negatively influenced and, as a result, locate the wrong Pletholand. Some who have erred have thought that a particular path led to a more rewarding Pletholand because of the perceived gains and fame such land holds for its travelers and, as a result, they lost sight of their original Pletholand. Many who started out well had missed it as a result of this; they allowed Arogoto to influence them. They failed to realize that wherever their divine Pletholand is, there lies their abundance no matter what others may think about it. The important thing is to stay on your Pletholand and not be distracted and you will be blessed and also be a blessing. There are others who originally found their Pletholand but moved from there as a result of the influence of others and regretted their action. For some, it was too late to recover, which is why it's important to check with Wisdom before making any move. Those who checked with Wisdom at every turn of their journey eventually made it through. One of the greatest fallacies of Arogoto is to make Pilgrims feel they are self sufficient at some point. They ignore Wisdom's instructions and guidance, and this eventually becomes their undoing. Never ignore the instructions of Wisdom," he affirmed. At this point, Glory closed His eyes to search for answers and, reaching deep within, invited Wisdom to be his guide. Not long after, Wisdom walked in and corroborated all that Mentor had already told him. He said to him, "Locating your 'Where' in life is very important for your journey on this Pilgrims Path. Many pilgrims are in the wrong 'Where' and as a result have made some very grievous mistakes on this path. You cannot put a fish on land and expect it to survive; its natural habitat is in the water, so it is with a pilgrim who is not in his natural habitat designed for him by the King. There is a place of function and impact for every pilgrim. That is the reason why no one is taken up to the Mountaintop Boulevard immediately after they have escaped from the gulag of Valleytown. There is a path to travel and there you will find your Pletholand." After Wisdom was done speaking, something stirred up in the heart of Glory which led to an awesome discovery.

What Lane

The walk through the Discovery Avenue had been an eye opener for Glory. Walking through the "Who Lane" had actually made him discover his true identity and who he is not. Moving through the "Why Lane" opened his eyes to why he was actually liberated from Valley-town, while the "Where Lane" made him realize there is a Pletholand for every pilgrim and pitfalls to avoid when discovering your Pletholand.

While Glory was busy ruminating about his experience so far, Mentor walked up to him and, with a pat on his shoulder and a smile lighting up his wrinkled face, told him they were about to take a walk through the "What lane." "This is the place of actual discovery. If after all the beautiful experiences and lessons you have learned from the previous lanes, you fail to discover the specifics of what it is you are actually supposed to do, then all your experiences and lessons learnt will amount to nothing at the end of the day. The 'What lane' is the place of discovering your specific assignment. Hence, this is a very crucial stage of your journey and your discovery here will determine the path of your journey. There is a single path that leads to the Mountaintop Boulevard but there are several 'link roads' attached to it. And every pilgrim will travel in specific 'link roads' on this path. As you walk through the 'What Lane,' you will be able to discover which of the 'link roads' you will be traveling in," He said.

Using himself as an example, Mentor said, "It was on this lane I was able to discover the specifics of what I was liberated to do. My name is connected to my assignment and that is why I have dedicated my time to help and encourage pilgrims as they journey through the Discovery Lane. I do this with so much joy and sense of urgency, too, because I found out that the time to walk through this path is short.

There are times during this assignment that I have been sad because I have seen situations where some pilgrims, after gloriously traveling through the Discovery Lane eventually ended up taking a detour back to Valleytown yielding to the deception of Arogoto." Mentor further revealed an insightful part of him to Glory. He said to him, "I did not just set out to become who I am. What I am doing now was something I grew into. It has taken many battles fought, many victories won and some blows and defeats encountered; all these are revealed on my armor as you can see. The dent and blood stains are the trophies I have earned in the course of my assignment and that is why I was renamed Mentor because that wasn't my name from the beginning. There are many people who bear the same name as me but only a few have the seal of approval from the King of the Mountaintop, and everyone will be accountable to Him at the end of our journey."

Glory, listening with keen interest, asked, "What other assignments are taken up by pilgrims as they journey through this path?" Mentor replied, "The pools of assignments are inexhaustible. A pilgrim should have no excuse why he should not be engaged in his niche. The King has endowed every pilgrim with special abilities for their specific assignments and, as a result, no one is inexcusable. There are pilgrims whose major niche is to encourage others by sharing their experiences and providing guidance just like what I am doing with you. There are others who provide refreshment to weary pilgrims as they journey through. Others are endowed with the gifts of understanding the times and mysteries of life and are able to decipher and help others by providing inspiration in this regard. Some are blessed with the gift of oratory and they come in handy to motivate pilgrims and stir them up to continue in this race and not be deterred. For some, it is the divine ability to use their voices as a tool for inspiration through deep songs that reach down to the very core of the heart." Mentor paused for a little while and, with a sad grin on his face, he said, "A lot of pilgrims who the King had blessed with these special abilities were eventually deceived by Arogoto, who used the bait of fame and wealth to entice them with the hope they would use these gifts for him. Many could not resist the pull and eventually, they took the detour back to Valleytown, and as a result, plundered their soul. This made the King sad and if only they could see what awaits them on the Mountaintop Boulevard, they would not have heeded to the antics of the proud one." He further said that there are others who have mastery of the manual and have been instrumental to using this ability to interpret this to other pilgrims. Mentor sounded a note of warning to Glory that he should be careful of some pilgrims who claim they have sound mastery of the manual and treasure map. "There are people who Arogoto has cornered and planted on this path. They are readily available to sway others by wrongfully interpreting the manual for their selfish gain. These people have been deceived already and they are looking for others to deceive." Mentor said. He reminded Glory to always check with Wisdom when it comes to what to accept and what not to believe. "There are many false interpreters of the manual. Thus, there is a need for caution as you travel through. Make Wisdom your standard and let Him be your check and balance. Although, it is expected for every pilgrim to understand how Arogoto operates and how he devices his mischief, there are some who, by constantly communicating with Wisdom, understand the wicked wiles of Arogoto better than others. These are people who have won a lot of victories simply by being in constant communication with Wisdom. Even though it is expected that we all communicate with Wisdom, there are pilgrims who have made it a lifestyle in this journey to do so and they have also helped others who have encountered struggles in their journey. They are constantly a threat to Arogoto and are also subject to constant and ferocious attacks from him, but because of their intimacy with Wisdom, they overcame. Although there had been a few instances where, as a result of carelessness, some of these warriors, as they are generally called, fell prey to the chief enemy of the pilgrims. For some it was a mortal blow while for others they were able, through the help of Wisdom and Mentors like me, to rediscover themselves." Mentor continued, "There are others who have been great representatives of the King at various frontiers in this part of the divide. They exude excellence and integrity because this is the lifestyle of the Kingdom and, as a result, bring glory to the King of the Mountaintop Boulevard."

After Mentor was done speaking, he took Glory by the hand and led him into an isolated room on the lane. The room could only hold a person at a time, making it impossible for Mentor to go in with Glory. This isolated room is called the Discovery Room. It is the place where pilgrims find their specific niche. Unfortunately, not every pilgrim goes through this room, despite traveling through the "What Lane." It is a place of solitary encounters. Mentor had done his bit by providing guidance and inspiration. The journey of a pilgrim actually discovering his niche is a solitary one. The length of time spent in the Discovery Room varies depending on how long it takes to discover the assignment; this could take years, but there have been occasions where a couple of hours did it and usually this is the case when the pilgrim is dependent and open to Wisdom. This was the case of Glory because it took him a few hours to exit the room. "I found it!" He exclaimed as he hugged Mentor. He said to Mentor, "What I experienced in the Discovery Room, I had never encountered such before. Something close to this experience was when I escaped from Valleytown and had the armor in exchange for all I had on then. In that Discovery Room, I found my assignment. I have been called to be a Warrior. I have been assigned to help other pilgrims confront the menace of Arogoto." Mentor, with a smirk on his face, said, "This is a serious assignment. The Pilgrims Path is a tortuous one. For you to be successful in this assignment, an extra level of commitment is requested of you, which means you have to stay on track and be focused and, at the same time, be a burden bearer for other pilgrims, particularly the weak ones." Glory responded, "I was made to understand that my experience with Arogoto and circumstances that surrounded my escape have prepared me for these tasks. Having served at the high echelon of Arogoto foot soldiers and the extent to which I went to acquire power, I was already exposed to the operations and cunning devices of how he operates. My communication with Wisdom has also prepared me to be a thorn in the flesh of Arogoto." Mentor, having heard all that Glory said, placed his hands on his shoulder and said, "You will succeed." He encouraged Glory, "Never fall for the subtle deception that you can execute your assignment without the help of Wisdom. You should also be careful of pride because many pilgrims who had the same assignment were struck with the arrow of pride and they bled until they died on this path. Glory, you may not understand the depth of what I just said until you move to the next phase of your journey. I am happy you have discovered yourself but there is still one more phase for you to go through to wrap up your journey through the Discovery Avenue." Mentor concluded.

When Lane

"Time is of the essence as you journey through the Pilgrims Path. There is timing for everything. The problem with many pilgrims is that they are so much in a hurry and as a result miss out in the King's timing." Glory, wondering whose voice it was that spoke, turned and saw it was Wisdom. Mentor said, "I will have to go, as there are others waiting for me, but do not hesitate to call me. I will be available whenever you need me. The journey through the 'When lane' must be taken alone with Wisdom because it is He who has the keys of the times." After Mentor had finished speaking, he hugged Glory and bade him goodbye. Wisdom moved closer to Glory, who was still reminiscing on the impact Mentor has on his life and said, "You are entering the lane that you will continue to travel in until you arrive at the bay of the Mountaintop Boulevard. It is a journey of patience and determination. A lot of things will unfold as you journey through." He continued by telling Glory, "To be successful, you must always consult with me as events unfold. There is a time connected to every single event in every pilgrim's life. Some have been so hasty that they leaped before their time and they missed it. On the other hand, others had experienced delays brought about by Arogoto with the intent of distracting them and making them lose faith in the manual and my guidance." He further said, "There is a priceless lesson to learn on the 'When Lane' and that is, to never allow the inordinate drive to want to catch up with the others to control you. Everyone's race is set in its path. When you faithfully stay on your track, you will one day become a beacon of encouragement to others and, like Mentor, other pilgrims will seek your counsel. Different events of your journey are connected to different times. You need to be in constant touch with me to understand these times. Some events will unfold in your timeline and unless you are constantly communicating with me, you will never realize these special events when they happen." He warned Glory, "Never be in a hurry, otherwise you may stumble and make mistakes that will make you sorry and some of this may be fatal as you may not be able to recover. Life is a process and the race to the Mountaintop should not be made in a hurry but rather, it should be done with patience. It is those who go the full haul that make it to the end. You must communicate with me constantly because it is through this I will be able to reveal the times and seasons to you. Just like you have different harvest times for different crops, so also, there are different times and seasons on the Pilgrims Path. A mango tree cannot be harvested at the same time as the maize. What good is it when you attempt to harvest a crop before it's time or to put it the other way? What good is it when fruits are left on the open field to rot away after the tedious planting season? That is how the life of a pilgrim is. When you manifest before your time, you will fizzle out within a short while and, when you are unable to decipher your time of manifestation, you'll become an 'obese' of a pilgrim, a 'dead sea' with so much stashed within but unable to make any impact on the Pilgrims Path."

Wisdom, fixing His gaze on Glory, said, "I have no doubt you will make it through, but you should be prepared for a rough journey because Arogoto has not given up on you or any other pilgrim for that matter. Stay away from envy, as this will put you under undue pressure. You must understand that people that compare themselves with others are not wise."

Raising the pitch of His voice, He said, "Don't run another man's race, stay on your track. There is no purpose that is the same, they may only be similar. Don't be pressured into doing what other pilgrims are doing because they are relatively successful in it. Always follow my lead and once you remain in my will, no matter how long it takes you will break forth. Everything is wrapped up in time. Be careful of the 'users and dumpers.' These are those who use you to achieve their own inordinate desires and, once this is achieved, they put you aside. Such people are not of the King. They are those who can do anything to make it at the expense of the King and of others. Be careful of such. They are busy building another kingdom that has no foundation in me. These are pilgrims but they are heading unto their perdition if they don't turn from their selfish ways. Such enjoy the company of men-praisers who urge them on; though many know they have deviated and abhor the company of those that will point them to the truth. Be careful of them, their path is slippery," warned Wisdom.

"Pride is a deadly arrow used by Arogoto to shoot at pilgrims. Oh! A lot of pilgrims who started well have been brought down by this. Pride is subtle. You might think you are humble but before the King, you are of a haughty heart. Many pilgrims feel they are so humble that this feeling of humility eventually becomes a snare unto them. The moment you become aware of your humility, you are already slipping into the zone of pride. The King resists the proud but He honors the humble. Many have usurped my position before the people. They have laid claim to their accomplishment without giving the King the honor. Glory, be warned! Many of these pilgrims received the warning with sobriety just like you but they became a target of the enemy, and they began enjoying a fair level of appreciation from others for the impact they are making on the Pilgrims Path, rather than returning the glory back to the King. It got into their head and the enemy saw this, took advantage of the moment and they began to slip away. At this time, they cared less about consulting me and even the manual became too old fashioned for them. Arogoto understands the importance of staying in touch with me and constantly consulting the manual for instruction and direction. He knows if he can succeed to cut the pilgrim off these, he will be able to alienate him unto himself and fulfill his desires on him," Wisdom said.

Glory, after soaking in all Wisdom had to share with him, with tears in his eyes promised Wisdom he will heed all the warnings and admonition given to him. He said, "The experiences of others have become lessons learnt and he will imbibe these as he continues on his journey." With this said, Wisdom pulled Glory close and embraced him, saying, "I will ever be close to you but for me to remain active in your journey, you should never fail to call on me and seek out the instructions in the Manual." Glory, with tears in his eyes, promised never to forget these truths revealed to him as they are the keys needed to navigate the rugged Pilgrims Path successfully. Wisdom said, "It is time to move on. My presence will go with you but when you need me, call me and I will be right there."

With these words, Wisdom left the presence of Glory whilst he took a look at the "When Lane" again, pondering over all that had happened to him on the Discovery Avenue. Slowly, he walked towards the exit with a will like steel to make it through the Pilgrims Path no matter the challenges that face him.

Chapter 4

The Battle at Middle-point

Glory was still engrossed in thought when he exited the Discovery Avenue. He was unaware of the fact that he had moved into a completely new terrain of his sojourn. As he walked, wandering on the Pilgrims Path, a bright light piercing through the leaves of a nearby tree helped jolt him back to consciousness. It was at this point he realized he was in the Wow Precinct.

Wow Precinct

The serenity of the Wow Precinct made Glory forget all the experiences he had been through. This, for him, was an entirely different experience. He began to enjoy the blessings of having gone through the Discovery Avenue. At the Discovery Avenue, he discovered his purpose among other things while on the Wow Precinct he began to live out that purpose. Glory was at peace with himself and hoped he could build a tabernacle in this precinct and end his journey there. His mixed experiences in Valleytown, as well as on his journey so far, made him an ideal figure for other weary Pilgrims to go to in their time of trials and tribulations. People looked up to him and his words spread abroad within the Pilgrims Path, even as far as Valleytown. There were instances where fellow Pilgrims were bruised on the path and while some pilgrims left them to bleed out the grace in them, others mocked and passed judgment on them, inferring that they were suffering for one wrong or the other. This was not the case with Glory, he would rally other pilgrims of like mind to give support to the wounded, and many pilgrims through such gestures were restored back to the path.

As Glory continued his journey on the Wow Precinct, he met with another pilgrim called Tahila who had a tattered armor on and who was bleeding out grace from all parts of his body. Tahila told Glory how he had been attacked by ravenous beasts sent against him by Arogoto and that things got worse for him when he chose not to journey through the Discovery Avenue. He said, "I was ignorant about what to expect, and the wicked one knew this and exploited it maximally to his advantage. I am paying dearly for that single mistake. I was warned by Wisdom not to continue the journey without going through the Discovery Avenue but I was confused when some other pilgrims I met on the path told me not to worry, that it was not a big deal if I chose not to, using themselves as examples. I went with the advice of the latter and my life had never remained the same afterwards. I have been a victim of manipulation, unfortunately by some pilgrims, and I have found it difficult to explain why some Pilgrims will put up such attitudes towards me. The greater evil is my being subjected to different attacks by Arogoto and his cohorts." Glory, being moved with compassion after listening to all that Tahila had to say, moved close and with eyes filled with love, Glory said, "It is not too late to make amends. Ignoring the counsel of Wisdom was your greatest undoing. Any pilgrim that does this will certainly end in perdition. Did you take time to read the pilgrim's manual?" Glory asked. "No," replied Tahila. "I was told by those I allowed to surround me that it was not important for my journey and that all I needed was to just look inward and I would find answers to every question that I have. They sounded so convincing and had power to sway with their words, such that a lot of fellow pilgrims have been deceived," he said. Glory placed his hands on Tahila's shoulder and said, "There are two very important things you must focus on in the course of your journey on this Pilgrims Path, one of which is the study of the manual; for in it contains the instructions on how to live and navigate through the Pilgrims Path. Reading the manual is not enough, you need to imbibe the principles therein; it is only then that you can be prepared to face any challenge on this path. The other thing is allowing Wisdom to have unrestrained access to every aspect of your life. When you give Him room, He will occupy your life. A lot of pilgrims have encountered problems because they have ignored the place of Wisdom and have outrightly rejected the instructions from the manual. My journey through the Discovery Avenue prepared and shielded me from some of the challenges you have gone through. All hope is not lost. It is not too late to make that trip through the Discovery Avenue and discover yourself. Once you discover yourself, the enemy will find it difficult to take advantage of you." Tahila responded, "I am willing to take this step. I have allowed myself to be manipulated by people, who told me it did not matter in the first place and I have sought the easiest and quickest route, or so I thought, but I have discovered that shortcuts are always the longest route. Now, I have no choice but to go back and travel through that path." Glory cut in, "Of course you have a choice, just like you had the first time, but always know that there are consequences for every choice that we make. I am glad you have made up your mind to go through the Discovery Avenue." Tahila further asked, "how do I understand all that will be showed or told to me, will I not require a tour guide?'" Glory responded, "It is a matter of choice again. You may decide to go through this alone or ask for guidance of another who has gone through this path before." Tahila thought about this for a while and said, "I will want to go on this journey alone. My past experiences with some pilgrims on this path have made me lose trust in people, and as such, I would like to embark on this journey to self discovery on my own. Glory advised, "You should not take the journey alone, but you can if you choose to. You will need the presence of either Wisdom or Mentor, or just the presence of Wisdom alone in your journey through the Discovery Avenue. I must also sound the note of caution; you should not embark on the journey with the guidance of Mentor without the presence of Wisdom. Every journey through the Discovery Avenue without the presence of Wisdom is a waste of time." Glory further shared his own experience with him and told him he has no doubt that discovering who he is will change his life and make his journey easier. With this said, they hugged one another, and while Tahila retraced his steps back, Glory was happy he was able to help a weary and wounded pilgrim. He said to himself, "I am now living out my purpose and have never enjoyed my journey through this path as much as I am right now."

Is This A Mirage?

While still reminiscing on his experience with Tahila, Glory felt a soft squeeze on his shoulder. When he turned around, he saw Wisdom standing behind Him with His face lit with a smile. He said, "You have done well, Glory, and I am happy you were able to help a weary pilgrim back onto his feet. Unfortunately, what you have done to Tahila is not common anymore on the Pilgrims Path. It used to be the case in the beginning but this is very rare now. What we see these days are pilgrims who should have helped Tahila but rather, they end up making things difficult for him; they castigate him and pass judgment on him. When this happens, many of the wounded will eventually 'grace-bleed' to death. Others will be swept off by the enticing pecks presented by Arogoto, and before you know it, they are gone with him. Some of these wounded pilgrims are jabbed at and turned into a laughing stock by their fellow pilgrims and the enemy sees these and provides them with a false shoulder to lean on; many of them are lured back into Valleytown and back into bondage because of the indifference and the lackadaisical attitude of fellow pilgrims. Many have been buried on this Pilgrims Path." Glory listened with rapt attention as Wisdom continued. He further said, "Many pilgrims started well on their journey but not everyone ends well (or will end well). Many of them missed it when they got to the Middlepoint. A lot of things happen at the Middlepoint; some pilgrims will have experienced great surges in their journey that they would become independent of my leading and instruction. They feel they have arrived and as a result become self sufficient in their journey without my guide, but alas! This has become one of the greatest undoing for pilgrims that get to this stage in their journey. Many have grown in influence such that they have taken over my role in the lives of other pilgrims. Very sad is the fact that many of the 'Super weight' pilgrims have merchandised my name. They will never offer to help pilgrims that will not help make them more visible to others. They will not go to pilgrims who are genuinely in need of the grace I have given to them and would rather go to those who will offer them gain in return for helping them. This is a grievous pandemic that has eaten into many of the so called 'super weight' pilgrims. I have reached out to them and sent fellow pilgrims to them but they have refused to listen and change. Glory, I need to let you know, they do not have my support. Many have drifted from the path and they are leading many young pilgrims astray by this act. Arogoto, who is never tired until he sees that pilgrims are recaptured and taken back to Valleytown, has devised means to lure the young pilgrims unto him. And since many young pilgrims relish the spotlight, Arogoto has offered them fame and power on a platter, whilst these young pilgrims are required to give him their hearts in return and have their final destination sealed unto perdition." Wisdom, looking into the eyes of Glory with a kind of piercing allure, said to him, "You must be very careful. Don't let the fame get into your head. Don't pay attention to people calling out your name and alluding great things to it such that it gets into you and you begin to see yourself without me. Don't let this happen to you, otherwise, this will be the beginning of the end for you and you may not live on this Pilgrims Path to tell your story. I have put my light in you and no doubt this will attract others to you because that is what my light will do, but when this happen, don't usurp what belongs to me. I own it all and I have given you a bit so you could be a blessing. When you are a blessing, it's definite that you must be blessed, but one thing I desire is for you to hallow my name. Let the pilgrims on the path know I am the one doing all that is manifesting through you. Also know that my light will attract attacks and rage from the arch enemy of the pilgrims. You must be prepared. Many have missed it at the Middlepoint. It is the place of battle. It is a hurdle you have to scale as you progress in your journey, which is why you must not be too comfortable to the point where you do not have your complete armor on. You must constantly be in touch with the manual. Always go back to the treasure map to make sure you are on the path. The manual and treasure map are guides for every pilgrim, but unfortunately, many may no longer be able to find the manual or the treasure map. Many have exchanged theirs for the fame and power that the arch enemy has promised them because Arogoto knows the power embedded in the manual and treasure map and will do everything to ensure that pilgrims do not keep theirs, and even if they do have it, he will do everything to ensure that they cannot access it. Many have lost theirs on this journey.

The enemies attacked them and they lost touch with the precious instructions in the manual. Be prepared for the enemy's attack because it will come and the essence is to make you lose focus and sense of direction. Some pilgrims feel they are abandoned by the King of the Mountaintop Boulevard and as a result, they throw away the manual and curse Him in the process. What I am telling you is what many of the 'super weight' pilgrims will not tell you or others. They make it seem it will be smooth all the way through and they make it seem like there will be more than enough cookies and sandwiches for you as you travel on this path. What they fail to tell you is that sometimes the road is lonely and sometimes you think you are the only one left on the path. They have exchanged my instructions of doggedness, commitment and consistency, which are requirements for making it to the mountaintop with the 'feel good annotations' that will only stir up emotions, but they will end up not sustaining them. For some pilgrims, it will be through much tribulation that they will make it to the Mountaintop."

Glory, having soaked in all that Wisdom told him, heaved a sigh and resting his tired frame on a pole by the side and said to Wisdom, "It's a tortuous path already and I wonder how many will eventually make it to the Mountaintop." Wisdom smiled and answered, "Not many will make it there despite the fact that the Mountaintop Boulevard is meant for everyone, but it is unsavory to note that not everyone will make it there. Quite a number of those on the Pilgrims Path will not make it there. The reason is this: it is a different lifestyle on the Mountaintop and the King can never compromise or lower His standards. A lot of pilgrims, and I mean many 'super weight' pilgrims, will not make it to the Mountaintop. This is a serious issue that has been discussed at the Council and a final agreement has been reached that the standard will never be compromised for anyone, no matter who it may be. So let no one deceive you. There is a standard set by the King and this must be followed to the letter. However, all through the Pilgrims Path are charging points where you can charge up your armor and replenish gracevine. Gracevine is very important for the race you have embarked on. It is a special favor from the King, available to everyone and even those in the gulag down in Valleytown are not exempted from this. Always ensure that your gracevine is fully charged. You will need this as you proceed in your journey. As you have observed, pilgrims that are wounded on this journey bleed out grace and if nothing is done to top their gracevine, many will not recover from the wound. You also have my ever abiding presence with you; call on me and I will be there. I cannot emphasize this more. Once again, never get to a level where you think you have achieved it all and you neither need me nor the manual in your journey. Those that do this are no more on this path. Be careful!" With these words, Wisdom pulled Glory closer to Him and wrapped His hands around him; a mighty surge like a current went through His body and he began to jerk and slipped into unconsciousness. By the time Glory regained consciousness, Wisdom had left. He picked himself up, and as he set out to continue his journey, he felt an unusual strength from within. He looked at his armor and ensured that every component of the armor was properly fitted. He also had his sword sharpened and held it in his hand as he approached the road called Bend.

The Rage and Raid

As he (Glory) moved on the road called Bend, he started hearing different alluring sounds; there were several of them with promises of a better opportunity if only he would commit to them. Right before his face were flashes of who he would become if he heeded to their enticement. He saw a lot of people bow before him, singing his praise. He saw himself with a rod in his hands and could not understand what this stood for. As if reading his thoughts, one of the voices spoke from the woods saying, "That will be your staff of authority if you commit to me." "Who are you?" Asked Glory - at this point he was taking it a step at a time. The voice responded, "I am he who has made many great and famous. I own this path and I dictate the life here. Don't think you can survive this grueling journey without my help. You need me. All you need to do is to accept my offer and I will show you a better route. It is stress free! It is the popular road. A countless number of people have gone through it, and your fellow pilgrims who accepted my offer are having the time of their lives. I am sure if I mention some of their names you will know them. Some of them are being regarded as the 'super weight' pilgrims of whom many look up to. I made them who they are. I gave them power and fame because they accepted me. There are some other so-called 'super weight' pilgrims that have a different kind of power, one they said was given to them by the King of the Mountaintop Boulevard, but that cannot be compared with the power I will give to you when you decide to become a part of my ever growing team. You will not have to struggle to gain access to this, as compared to the power you get from the King which will require you to make sacrifices and a very high degree of commitment to be entrusted with such power, but I will make it easy for you. You will not have to struggle before you get this. All I need from you is just for you to accept my offer and you leave the rest to me." Whilst Glory listened to all that was said, the motion pictures of what he supposedly stood to gain if he eventually accepted the offer kept playing right in front of him. While this happened, the personalities from the woods showed up. Their appearances were quite intimidating and every one of them held a glittering staff in their hands. They had faces that were without blemish and spoke with soft voices to Glory, who was already awe- stricken by their presence. His mind was beginning to play along with all that he had been told. He was beginning to give it a thought. He thought to himself, "Perhaps this is true. I can accept their offer and still continue on the Pilgrims Path that leads to the Mountaintop. At least they said there are a lot of the 'super weight' pilgrims who have done the same and are enjoying this same privilege. I have labored and I have gone through so much, and this may be the opportunity that will change things for me for the rest of my life. I know there is a way this can be managed collectively. I am sure there are pilgrims I can consult with who have been able to manage successfully the combination of this offer with their journey on this path. I have heard them say it. Maybe I should give it a try." While Glory was engrossed in his thoughts, one of the voices called out to him and said, "Don't worry, Glory, we will not leave you by yourself to do this alone. We will be here to guide you and make it easy for you. We have pilgrims, and I mean the 'super weight' pilgrims, that you can consult for advice if you need to be convinced. In fact, their appearances alone will tell you what you stand to benefit. You will see the glitz and glamour around them, and this will certainly convince you, no doubt. And remember, this will not stop you from your journey to the Mountaintop Boulevard. Glory answered in the affirmative the need to seek out one of the 'super pilgrims' they would recommend. They suggested he go talk to 'Lord Superior' and told him where he could be found. They even offered to facilitate the meeting as they said it is usually not easy getting a hold of him because of his very busy engagements, but they can facilitate an easy and quick access.

True to their word, they arranged a meeting between the Lord

Superior and Glory. Glory was awe struck when he met Lord Superior because this was one of the highly regarded 'super pilgrims' on the path. The opulence and the glitz, the intimidating personality and the entourage made up of other pilgrims struck a chord in the heart of Glory. He wanted the same. Everything he saw of the Lord Superior, he desired. Without even engaging in a conversation with him, he liked what he saw. He saw other pilgrims bow to him and how they held him in great reverence, and he in return relished every bit of it. "Hello, Glory! It's so good to see you. I have been told you desired to see me," said the Lord Superior. "Yes," replied Glory. "I have come to seek your counsel as directed by him who made you rich and famous." At this point, the Lord Superior asked to be left alone with Glory. He then gave a piercing look in the direction of Glory and said, "If you desire what I have, then you must be willing to pay the price that I paid. I desire and pray that my journey will end at the Mountaintop Boulevard, but I also realized when I started out on this journey, that it was a tortuous one for me. I fought battles like no other, and oftentimes I was isolated by the other pilgrims. Even though, Wisdom was there each time I needed him, I still felt the need to belong and be loved and appreciated, but unfortunately, my fellow pilgrims did not offer me that solace. In my isolation, I cried, but my mind was made up to make it through. I had the manual with me and regularly consulted it for guidance and inspiration. The sight of the treasure map kept hope alive in me. I have been tutored in the art of trickery of Arogoto and I was not ready to give up. I said to myself, "If my fellow pilgrims will ostracize me for a reason I cannot seem to fathom, I will continue in my walk on this path regardless of whatever happens." It was in this situation I heard of the 'super weight' pilgrims, the power that they wield and the strong influence they have over other pilgrims. They have been able to garner respect from others and when they speak, they get the attention of the people. From my findings, I discovered that many of these 'super weights' have been on this Pilgrims Path for a while; they are very experienced and many belong to the Mentor Family. I made up my mind, I was going to make my way up and become like one of them. I wasn't so interested in what some of them had done to get to this point of their walk on this path." At this point, Glory was soaking in every bit of what Lord Superior was saying. "All I was interested in," continued Lord Superior, "was just to become like one of them and enjoy the same privileges they have created for themselves. I must state also that even though we all are traveling on the same Pilgrims Path, our journeys differ from one another. Some may have similar experiences while others are completely different. I am sure there are experiences you've had that I haven't and vice versa, but in my early days, my desire was to become one of the 'super weight' pilgrims. In my quest to achieving that, I had an encounter with the Janitor." "Is that his name? He introduced himself as the one who has made many great and famous," Glory cuts in. "Yes, that is his name," replied Lord Superior. "He doesn't introduce himself as Janitor to people when he comes in contact with them for the first time. You have to have moved in just like the way you have done for you to be able to know him more. But there is something I can tell you, he delivers on his promise. He will certainly make you great and famous. I cannot begin to describe all that I have enjoyed after my encounter with the Janitor. My lack of security and my feelings of being neglected had all become a thing of the past. I am now being revered and appreciated. I have other pilgrims who now look up to me and want to be like me, but the truth is that not everyone who desired to be like the 'super weight' pilgrims would achieve this feat. In fact, very few will be called by that name." "Where is the place of Wisdom in all of this," asked Glory. The Lord Superior gave a long pause, and with a sigh, muttered "I lost Him." Glory, surprised at what the Lord Superior said, asked him, "What did you just say?" "I lost Him," repeated Lord Superior. "You know, you can't have both. I tried to juggle both worlds but I discovered it's not possible to combine both, but no one knows this until they are locked in. Not even the closest pilgrim to me knows this and I don't know why I am telling you this because I am not meant to do so. Everybody out there still thinks and feels that I am very much on track but I know that I have soiled my conscience. I have exchanged my convictions for fame and opulence. Within the pilgrim's community, I am still the highly revered Lord Superior, but I know there is a disconnect already. I need to let you know that very few of the 'super weight' pilgrims are still very much on track and have not drifted from the path. They are revered also, but the difference is that they have gone through the 'process' for them to get to this position. Their route is sometimes characterized by tears, loneliness, scars, battles, and through many tribulations, they have been made strong and prepared for this position. Theirs is a long and tortuous path, but if you come through the route of the Janitor, it is quick and easy, and that is why a lot of the 'super weights' have chosen this easy and quick path. It is a matter of choice. I have told you my heart and have gone ahead to let out secrets I haven't told anyone before, and I may pay dearly for this but I believe there is a purpose for this and I see the hand of the King of the Mountaintop involved in all of these things. I perceive you have a special assignment to help pilgrims seek out what is true and I still sincerely crave to return back to the true path, but there is a serious battle within me. What I stand to lose when I renounce the Janitor and all his allures and the shame and the fear of what will befall me after. These are silent torments within. Forget the facade that I put out there. I am sure the King of the Boulevard will not be satisfied with me and I desire also to make it eventually to the Mountaintop Boulevard." Glory, still reeling with shock, burst into tears, held the hands of Lord Superior and assured him, it was not too late for him to make amends and retrace his steps. Lord Superior quietly shrugged Glory off and with a sublime look said, "You don't really understand, it is deeper than this. I have given my soul in exchange for the glamour and the fame and I have been promised humiliation and eventual death if I try to renege on my part of the agreement. It is too late for me, but you can make up your mind not to entangle yourself because once you get in, it is difficult to get out. I

The Battle at Middle-point

am at a loss to why I am sharing these secrets with you because I am not supposed to tell you all these, but deep down in me, I have no regret even though I might be paying a price for this like I already told you." Glory, not giving up, said, "I believe you can still recharge your gracevine and get back on track. There might be a price to pay but you will eventually find peace and joy at the end of your journey on this Pilgrims Path. If you would not mind, I would want us to consult Wisdom because I know He is the only one that could help at this point in time. I was almost swayed myself but I know there is a purpose for every challenge we might be facing as pilgrims. It is important we understand that, because if we don't, then it is easy for Arogoto and his cohorts to make a mess of such pilgrims. We should understand that it was enough blow for Arogoto to have lost us to the King in the first place. I know him and I had served him relentlessly while in Valleytown, and I know he doesn't give up easily. He usually strikes when you least expect. He will fight until the very last and give the hot chase with the hope that he might succeed in winning you back. He is very subtle in the scheme he employs to achieve this. The janitor is one of his stooges he uses for this purpose. Lord Superior, I have gained insight into what you shared with me and I would rather be patient and learn through the process as the King has it laid out from the beginning than be in a craze-frenzy for what the Janitor is offering."

Glory continued, "I know with my decision, the battle line has been drawn and the Janitor and his enablers will come out voraciously in attack against me, but I am confident that since I survived Arogoto at the beginning, I will also overcome them, but my concern is for you." Whilst Glory was still speaking, Wisdom showed up with tears in His eyes, and whilst gazing in the direction of Lord Superior, said to him, "I didn't give you that name, there is no one that is Lord Superior other than the King of the Mountaintop Boulevard Himself. You were given the name that is exclusive to the King and Arogoto though his stooge knows this, he has always tried to usurp what belongs to the King and this is what set the King against him in the first place. I have reached out to you many times. I have tried to gain your attention but you were distracted; the fame, glitz and glamour became a noise that choked my voice. You became an overnight star through the help of the Janitor. I know all things and I know whoever has been helped to this height by the janitor does not finish well. They never make it through to the Mountaintop. I am sure you don't know this, most of the pilgrims that got their fame from the Janitor were lured into the 'detour' that eventually takes them back to Valleytown without them even knowing it. This is done in a very subtle manner and they will not realize it until they are back in the gulag. If only you can decide to renounce the Janitor and all his allurement, I will help you. I have always been there and am ready to help only if you will reach out to me. Whatever the Janitor has given to you is just smoke; it will fizzle out and you will be forgotten before you know it. It is a bait to drag you back into that terrible pit in Valleytown. All I require of you is for your mind to be made up because I cannot force you to accept what I am saying to you but I can strengthen you and be by your side all the way. Don't be distracted, I have the keys to genuine fame and honor such that will outlive time." Lord Superior was literally shaken when he listened to Wisdom speak. He was confused because he was torn between both worlds. For a moment, the glitz and fame he had enjoyed flashed before him. He saw how people had held him in high esteem, and how he had been highly revered. He thought about what other pilgrims would say about him when they eventually got to know about what happened. He thought about the battles with the Janitor and Arogoto for breaking the agreement. He looked up to Wisdom and said with misty eyes and with a choke in his voice, "I will stick with you, Wisdom. I know I have missed it and I am willing to make amends. My escape from Valleytown was driven by my desire to make it to the Mountaintop Boulevard. I risked everything for this at the very beginning, turned my back on friends and family who tried to stop me and now I have allowed what kept me as a slave of Arogoto in the first place to find its way back into me in a very subtle way. I never knew this is how far I would drift. I have been swayed and enticed by the promise of glamour and recognition, and of which truthfully I did receive, but I have now realized that this fame and all its pecks are simply a garnished bait to take me back to that dark hole." He looked in the direction of Glory, who was staring into the open space and was in awe of what was happening right in front of him and said, "Thank you Glory, for crossing my path and for not giving up on me. I am a changed pilgrim because you persevered. Even after I told you details, I should not have ordinarily revealed to you, you did not seek out help for yourself but you stayed through with me and invited Wisdom, who completed what you have started." While he was still speaking, Glory ran towards him and hugged him; they both wept on each other's shoulders.

Wisdom walked towards them and hugged both of them, and as he did, something like a gold cowry and bracelet fell from Lord Superior into the hands of Wisdom and he hugged them again and a surge of current went from him to both of them until they slipped into unconsciousness. When they regained consciousness, Wisdom was there waiting and He said to Lord Superior, who was still looking dazed, "Your name will now be Reignard and not Lord Superior. I will always be around you even though sometimes it may not seem like it. When you reach out to me, I will be here for you. You need to be strong because the Janitor will come out strong against you, but I can assure you that he will fail as long as you keep your focus on me. You need to dust and pick up the manual once again. You have lost track of the treasure chest; it's time to search it out and retrace your steps back from this route to the true path. It won't be easy, but I will be there with you." He looked at Glory, and with his hands placed on his shoulder, he nodded as if affirming something, and without saying a word, he walked away through the door.

Reignard walked up to Glory again and hugged him, thanking him for all that just happened to him and saying to him, "I was meant to win you over but you eventually had it reversed. I am grateful." Glory's face lit up and he said, "It's time to get back on the battle field; you must clad yourself in the full armor. I am sure the Janitor will not be smiling when he comes calling." Reignard said, "I will need a helping hand with my armor as it's been a long time now since I last used any of it. The Janitor made me believe I did not have need of it since I was the Lord Superior and this has made me lose touch with my armor. I have kept it aside and it has gathered dust over the years. I will need to clean it up and have it properly fitted back onto me." Glory watched as Reignard reached back for his armor and had it cleaned up by himself, after which he placed it on himself with the help of Glory, making sure everything was properly fastened. Glory said, "It is time for us to leave. We all must walk our walk and fight our battles but at this stage, I will need to stick with you so we can face the battle together. With the two of us together, it will be a formidable force against the Janitor and his stooges, not forgetting that Wisdom is also with us.

They both advanced together and as they came out, they met the Janitor at the entrance. He looked at Reignard in disbelief and said, "I am sure I am not seeing right. Did you see Lord Superior?" He asked. "You mean did I see Reignard?" He responded. "Who is Reignard? That is a strange name," responded the Janitor. "I am. The one you called the Lord

Superior has been renamed Reignard because whatever you do, this will not stop me from reigning with the King on the Mountaintop. And lest I forget, thank you for sending Glory my way, it eventually turned out to be the best thing you have done for me." As he said this, Glory stepped out of the shadows. They both could literally see the anger that welled up in the Janitor. He raised his hands, and with his head looking upwards and gave a shrieking yell, his eyeballs had turned red and he fixed his eyes on them and uttered words in a strange language. Balls of fire came out of his mouth with such a great power and hit Reignard with such force that it threw him against the tree and about the same time, balls of fire with arrows were directed at Glory, but he had his shield well in position and was shielded from the attack. He ran and lifted up Reignard, who was still reeling in pain from the attack. The balls of fire had created a dent on his breastplate and he was struggling to stand when Glory rushed and gave him a helping hand. Reignard said, "I didn't know what hit me. It happened so fast that before I could pull my shield, I was already on the ground. It was like I became blinded by the blast from the fire." While he was speaking, the Janitor had asked for and received re-enforcement, and he had a large host with him as it were prepared for battle. Reignard had regained his full balance at this stage. His armor was now fully intact with his sword drawn and shield in place and Glory having done the same turned towards Reignard and said, "We are no match for this army. Our strength will fail. They will overrun us." He closed his eyes and spoke some words, and by the time he opened his eyes. Wisdom was there with them, clad in a brazen fiery armor. Glory had never seen Wisdom clad in armor before. The closest he saw of him clad in a similar situation was when he intervened in his escape from Valleytown. Wisdom turned to them and said, "You will not need to fight in this battle. For as long as you have called me to step in, I will take over your battles." While he was speaking, the Janitor and his cohorts charged towards them with great rage." Wisdom still kept talking to Glory and Reignard as if ignoring the enemy advancing towards them, saying, "Stay with me! Don't let their presence intimidate you. Stay with me and keep your focus on me and not the raging battle." The Janitor and his army were some inches away when Wisdom suddenly turned towards them and immediately there was a whirlwind that ensued which blew the Janitor and cohorts far away from them. They could hear the shrieking scream of the enemy until it faded. Glory could not believe what had just happened. It was a great relief for the both of them. He had discovered a new secret, deciding to fight your battles yourself is your choice. Wisdom corroborating Glory's position said, "Many pilgrims have lost battles, many have been forcefully pulled off the Pilgrims Path because they feel they are sufficient by themselves to face Arogoto and his annoying armies. There are battles that your mortal minds cannot withstand and an attempt to forge ahead will turn you into a puppet of Arogoto. Some pilgrims have been engaged in fighting battles all through their journeys. I understand the Pilgrims Path is full of battles but some are unnecessary if only you have fully followed the instruction laid out in the manual and sought out my presence. That is why I am here, to make the burden on this Pilgrims Path light enough for you to bear, but unfortunately, many pilgrims have lost sight of these truths; believing they could do this and engage the enemy by themselves. The resultant effect is that many of these pilgrims eventually will become frustrated and will lose the zest to continue on this path making them easy prey for the army of Arogoto." Wisdom further said to Glory, "You have come this far because you have learnt these secrets and you have obeyed the instructions you have seen within the manual. Continue to run your race, you are almost there. The

King of the Mountaintop Boulevard is happy for the progress you have made. The journey is not over yet; there are still battles ahead. Now you know the secrets of how to overcome your battles, never forget this; you don't have to fight your battles when I am here to bear your burdens. All you need to do is to reach out to me, seek me out and I will be there for you. I hear pilgrims' grumbled saying that they sought my presence when they came face to face with the enemy but I did not show up. The truth is, I was there but they could not see me. I could see them but there were fogs created by the enemy but allowed by them to obstruct their view of me, and at other times, I had come to strengthen them to go through that battle unscathed." Turning His gaze on Reignard, He said, "It's time for you to take your place on the Pilgrims Path. I am glad you have retraced your steps back. You have heard all I said. For you to succeed in your journey, you must never think you are now sufficient by yourself and as such you do not need me. I am the Light on this path and when you stick with me, I will light up your path." Reignard walked towards Wisdom, knelt down and wrapped his hand around Him. Wisdom in turn laid His hands on Reignard's helmet. He lifted up His eyes and there was a glow that emanated from Him and covered Reignard, and immediately

Glory saw what was happening. He ran towards them and knelt beside Reignard, and he was also covered in the glow. Wisdom looked at Glory and said, "You have done something that is not common anymore among the pilgrims. Many have created their own space and rather for them to fellowship and get involved to help and encourage one another, they have separated themselves from fellow pilgrims and tagged genuine experiences like what just happened now as strange fire, but the truth is the pride of their heart, the 'super weight' pilgrim mentality has eaten deep into the fabric of their soul. I see all these. The King beholds all these with pain in His heart. He has told me many times how pained He is to see His pilgrims avoid one another like a plague. There is no segregation on the Mountaintop. The life there is that of warmth and friendliness. I see these things and I know the hearts of everyone and I will establish my judgment based on the motive behind the actions of the pilgrims. I see the deepest part of the heart, even the one that is not open to the pilgrim himself. And don't get me wrong, I know there are pilgrims who have been corrupted and they are out to do same to others. When this is the case, then we know what to do base on what the manual instructs, but let us not disdain one another. Many of my genuine 'super weight' pilgrims have garnered for themselves a huge cult-like following and this has bred differentials among the pilgrims and, unfortunately, many have swayed attention unto themselves and not the King of the Boulevard anymore. Their emphasis has now changed from telling the pilgrims about my standards to how easy they can live their lives on the Pilgrims Path, showing them other routes that will only lead the pilgrims and themselves into the pit. I will judge all these and I will not compromise my standard. The Mountaintop council has reached that final verdict; no pilgrim, no matter the clout, will be allowed passage onto the Mountaintop if the standard has been compromised. My standards are not hidden; they have been spelt out in simple terms in the manual." At this stage, Reignard and Glory stood up with Reignard placing his hand on Glory's shoulder and said, "Thank you for the help and sacrifice you have made, thank you." Wisdom was already gone from them. Glory said, "We must continue our journey. Each one will have to walk his walk but I will be here if you need someone to talk to, but remember all Wisdom told us and always consult Him; you don't have to be in trouble to do this. Make it a regular habit to seek Him out. He will be found of you when you do. I am happy you have dusted your manual; as you rightly know, embedded in it is the treasure map that has the details of how to find the treasure chest located on the Mountaintop Boulevard. I hope we meet up again on this Pilgrims Path but if we don't, I will look out for you when I arrive at the Mountaintop because my mind is made up; come what may, I will get to that Boulevard." With this said they hugged each other and bade goodbye, with Glory walking towards the pool.

The Pool of Refreshing

Glory continued his journey and approached a gate that had the inscription, "Welcome to the Pool of Refreshing." The gate opened of its own accord and Glory walked in. He laid down his armor, including his sword and shield, and took a dive into the pool. After spending some time in the pool, he felt strengthened and at the same time peaceful. It was such a feeling that would make any pilgrim want to remain in the pool for as long as possible. "Why didn't I know about this pool?" Glory muttered to himself. "The serenity will leave a pilgrim in awe," he continued. While he spoke to himself, Mentor walked in. This was the same Mentor that led him through the Discovery Avenue. He was glad to see Glory after such a long while. He walked into the pool and said to Glory, "I have been following up with your progress and I am so happy to know how much you have grown as you have journeyed along. I have come across pilgrims and only a few of them have been able to go this far to make the impact that you have made. I know of your encounter with Tahila and your most recent involvement with the Lord Superior, who is now called Reignard. You are living out your purpose and I am happy to see the progress you have made over this period of time," he said. Glory, beaming with a smile, answered, "I am glad our paths crossed and thank you for your counsel at the early stage of my journey, particularly my journey through the Discovery Avenue. The lessons learnt there have helped me in no small measure in my walk on this path. I sometimes wonder how my journey would have been if I had not gone through the experience I had at the Discovery Avenue." Mentor replied, "It is my joy to always see Pilgrims make progress in their journey. The goal is to see as many pilgrims as possible make it eventually to the Mountaintop Boulevard and in the process of doing that, we also strive daily in our walk on this path to make it. That is why you see me at the Pool of Refreshing." Glory responded, "Talking about the pool, there is this peace and tranquility that comes with this place. I also feel some sort of strength resurge through my entire body after staying in the pool for some time. I wonder why I hadn't known about this pool before now." Mentor smiled and said, "The pool is strategically positioned away from the hustle and bustle of the Pilgrims Path and located in this serene place to allow weary pilgrims to refresh and energize so they can continue on their journey. This is a provision made by the King himself. He knows the battles and rigors encountered by the pilgrims and have placed this pool here for us. Unfortunately, not many pilgrims utilize this provision. Many have been so battered that they cannot imagine that provisions exist. Others are so proud that they think they do not need to visit the Pool of Refreshing, while for some, it is just ignorance; an ignorance that is avoidable if only they had been reading the manual. There is still so much in the manual that you have not discovered; you have to constantly study the manual. Reading it is not enough. You know, there is the treasure map for the treasure chest in this manual and if you must know, the treasure chest contains countless treasures; engrafted in this treasure map are keys and codes required to unlock these treasures. Now, there is a secret I have discovered that has helped me in my personal journey on this Pilgrims Path. The more keys and codes I was able to discover, the more I was able to gain access into the treasure chest and uncover the treasures that have helped me become a better pilgrim. Let me correct an erroneous belief that I have found as we journey along; many pilgrims believe the treasure map is only for the treasure chest located on the Mountaintop, but this is not completely true. There are many treasures buried along the Pilgrims Path for our benefits in this journey, but many pilgrims are so focused on the grand treasures on the Mountaintop that they ignore the ones the King has made available for our use and convenience here." Glory was stunned by the exposition made by Mentor, as this was an eye-opener for him. He had believed that the treasure chest contained only treasures that were found on the Mountaintop, but from what he just heard, he could also benefit by discovering codes and keys for the treasures buried along the path. "Just listening to you again and receiving this great insight from you makes the Pool of Refreshing a worthwhile visit and I am glad our paths have crossed again," Glory said. Getting out of the pool, he felt as if he had received some energy shots. He picked up his shield and sword, waved goodbye to Mentor and continued his journey, feeling so excited about his new discovery.

Chapter 5

Journey Through Graveland#

I Like it Here

The recent experiences for Glory had been quite remarkable. His experience at the Pool of Refreshing energized him, as he felt renewed and invigorated. As he continued on the Pilgrims Path, he could perceive he was being seen differently by other pilgrims. He noticed a kind of reverence in their look. While he was still trying to coordinate his thoughts, one of the pilgrims walked up to him. "Are you Glory?" he asked. Glory, surprised, answered in the affirmative. "How do you know me?" replied Glory. "You are a popular name on this path and I have heard so much about you, particularly on how you've helped other pilgrims through their difficult times, and I would love to learn from you." Glory obliged his request and shared with him salient details that would help him on his journey. He shared the story of how he has been able to stay strong and focused in his journey. He said, "My journey has not been smooth altogether but I have learned the secrets to maintaining a keen focus. It is easy for you to get distracted on this path, as there is so much noise around. The arch enemy and his cohorts understand the use of distraction as a weapon, and he has used it effectively and succeeded in pulling down many pilgrims. This is a subtle strategy employed by him over the ages. Many have fallen flat because they have failed to train their focus. When we keep our focus on where we are heading, which for us is the Mountaintop, all other things along our journey will not have meaning to us, but I can tell you that this is a difficult thing to keep up with. Hence, our utmost need for Wisdom. He has been my Great Companion and without Him, I wouldn't have come this far. Those that ignored Him did so to their own peril. He has been there from the very beginning of my journey and I have learned to listen and obey Him." "Obedience is key," interjected the pilgrim. "Yes! It is," Glory affirmed. "Obedience to the Instructions laid out in the manual, and also to the counsel of Wisdom, is very important as we journey along. I have seen pilgrims who have completely discarded the manual. I have heard many say the instructions therein are no more relevant to our journey.

Some had tried to revise the manual so as to accommodate their wantonness. They were deceived and lured by Arogoto to do his bidding and they paid dearly with their lives. There has never been a manual that has been in use across generational boundaries except for the manual we have been given for this journey. Every effort to wipe out and destroy the manual has failed and will continue to fail." The pilgrim with whom he talked looked at him and, amazed by his depth of knowledge, said, "I did not do a proper introduction. My name is Precious. I have been on this journey for quite a while and I have gone through a lot of ups and downs and at a point took the sharp detour on the way back to Valleytown, but here I am again with another opportunity on this path, and I am blessed to have come across you as your counsel has been of help to me. I have suffered setback on my journey because I did not follow the instruction in the manual and I have learnt not to repeat the same mistake. Your counsel has helped to strengthen my resolve, so thanks for being a blessing to us." Glory smiled and said, "I am glad to be of help to fellow pilgrims and hearing this from you encourages me to do more." About this time, Glory discovered he could see beyond what others could see naturally. He was able to discern what was wrong with others by just looking at them. This made other pilgrims come and seek for counsel and help from him. Glory began to relish in the attention he received as more and more pilgrims began to seek him out.

The Highland of Fame

Glory progressed in his journey and came to a steep land called the Highland of Fame. There were quite a number of people here, but this land was so steep that people tended to slide from it and crash to the foot of the highland. It is not uncommon to see people jostling to get to the Highland of Fame. People on this highland have a kind of cult following. They are somewhat being worshipped and held in very high regards by others. For everyone who gets to this highland of fame, they receive tags that display their achievement. Some had multiple tags with bold inscriptions of what they have done and achieved to earn a spot on the highland. Another surprising thing is that no one remains on this highland for very long. For some, as they are getting to feel the highland, they suddenly slip and fall off. They completely forget they are on a steep and slippery land, and whilst they relish in the tags they have received, they walk to the edge and before long, they are gone. There is also a link road called the Detour. This road is a beautiful and well-terraced path but a very slippery one too that leads back to Valleytown

This was where Glory found himself. He had on him various tags that attracted other pilgrims to him. He had been a great counselor to many, someone you could go to with your challenges and be rest assured you will find help. He had fought some of the fiercest battles on the Pilgrim's Path and had overcome. He has scars to show for the many travails he has been through. He is known to enjoy a wonderful relationship with Wisdom. He is deeply rooted in the knowledge and interpretation of the manual. He's been many things to different pilgrims. They looked up to him with great respect, and at a point they began to revere him, with some having his name imprinted on their armor. Some went further to compose songs about him. They held him in great esteem. For others, they felt he was the voice of Wisdom and whatever he said was accepted as a word from Him. Before long, pilgrims stopped seeking out Wisdom directly and were content with everything said by Glory. He relished the attention and enjoyed the spotlight. He was, for a time, who you would call the number one pilgrim on the Pilgrims Path.

He got so busy that he hardly searched the manual anymore, and for a very long time did not consult with Wisdom. He was beginning to drift towards the Detour. He couldn't see clearly as thick fog had formed. Each time people sang his praise, pockets of fog formed around him. Overtime, his vision became obscured so that he could not see clearly anymore. Unknown to Him, He started branching off towards the path that lead to the road called Detour.

The Detour

Glory continued on the Highland of Fame until his sight began to grow dim. He had branched off and entered through to the Detour, and because he could not see clearly anymore, he thought he was still on the Pilgrims Path that led to the Mountaintop. Suddenly, he lost traction and struggled for a while to regain his composure, but unfortunately, the ground was slippery and he began to slide. The slide was so rapid. The fog that had obstructed his vision was gone. His praise singers were nowhere to be found. All the tags he had on his armor were gone. He was alone and sliding deeper on the road to Detour. He began to hear noises which got louder as he slipped deeper. Later, the noises he heard became distinct voices similar to the language of those who live in Valleytown. It suddenly dawned on him that he was on his way back to Valleytown. He wanted to stop but could not. The ground became more slippery and the voices of people yelling and screaming became louder. He began to cry and suddenly, as if a scale fell off his eyes, he saw shoots and branches on both sides of the road. He managed to raise his hand to grab one of the shoots, but as soon as he touched it, it pricked his fingers. It was then that he realized the shoots had thorns on them. He kept sliding and the voices became louder. Streams of thoughts raced through his mind. He thought of his horrendous experience while he was in Valleytown; he remembered his escape and the price he paid. He thought of his early days on the Pilgrims Path and his encounter with Mentor and those wonderful moments of fellowship and interaction with Wisdom. He wondered how he found himself in this situation. He thought, "What happened to me? How could I degenerate so much that I am now on my way back to that gulag called Valleytown?" These questions raced through his mind in torrents. He wept! With his eyes closed and his right hand raised, he suddenly felt his hand hold a branch, only this time; it had no thorns on it. His downward slide stopped and when he opened his eyes, he saw he had held onto the branch of the Mercy Tree. He held onto the branch so firmly. He knew every attempt to let go of the Mercy Tree would spell doom for him. He held onto the branch because he knew his continued survival is tied to this. He noticed that the voices from beneath had ceased and everything had suddenly become silent.

And whilst he was still probing in his heart, he saw a light and someone walking towards him in the brightness of the light. As the person got closer, the light got more intense, such that Glory could not keep his eyes open. After a while, the footsteps ceased and Glory opened his eyes; standing right in front of him was Wisdom. Glory wept when he saw Wisdom, who gave him a hand and raised him up in his sliding position. Glory hugged Him and wept more on his shoulders. Wisdom looked at him with eyes full of compassion and said, "You are fortunate you found and held onto the Mercy Tree. Not many pilgrims are this fortunate." "What happened to you?" Wisdom asked. "I was watching you from afar. You built other walls around you, which made it difficult for me to reach you. You replaced my companionship with your own sufficiency, literally exposing yourself to what just happened to you. You began to play the role only reserved for me in the lives of other pilgrims and before long; they began to see you as me and would not even bother to consult me anymore. The Highland of Fame you went through was not meant to destroy you, but so many pilgrims could not manage their sojourn through this highland; many tripped and fell off the highland and plunged their soul. Many branched into the road called Detour as you did and never survived. They were in denial of what was happening to them. They were completely blinded by all the accolades they received from other pilgrims. Very few have been fortunate enough to rediscover themselves and make the journey back to the Pilgrims Path simply because they realized where they had failed and held unto the Mercy Tree before it was too late," He said. Glory broke down and wept all the more after he'd listened to Wisdom speak. He said, "Looking back, I detest every moment I'd been in that spotlight. I did not manage the situation well. I was careless. I allowed the privilege I had to get into me. I got so carried away that I failed to consult with you any longer. My manual was beginning to gather dust. I thought I had gone past the level of reaching out to you and searching out my manual for direction and instruction. It was a mistake that has cost me dearly and I regret every bit of my action." Raising his head and with his voice still shaky, he said, "Although this is an unpleasant experience for me, I am thankful I survived it even though I am not completely out of the hole yet. I know this experience will help in my continued journey on the Pilgrim Path. It's a lesson I have learnt and I will share with other pilgrims my experience, and hopefully some will learn a lesson or two from this. I will never neglect my manual anymore. It's been a most reliable guide. Thank you, Wisdom. Thank you for coming for me. I would have been lost and all works and efforts forgotten. I will never ignore you again. Whether Arogoto and his cohorts like it or not, I will make it to the Mountaintop. I want to see the King of the Boulevard, I want to embrace the Prince Charming and through your help I will make it," he said.

The Rediscovery

Wisdom moved closer to Glory, who was now sitting under the Mercy Tree. He pulled him up and said, "It's time to retrace your steps. You know what is required of you. You have learned from your experience. It is now time for you to focus on the rest of your journey. No matter what privileges and accomplishments you have received on the Pilgrims Path, this will pale in comparison to the ultimate fulfillment that will be experienced on the Mountaintop. Let the remainder of your journey be focused on staying on track. The lessons you have learned should be lived out on the path. It is no longer about you anymore. Shun the accolades; you may not be able to survive another crash. Point the people to me. Send them back to their manual. It is not about you anymore. If you do these things, I have no doubt you will make it through." With this said, Wisdom took Glory's hand and led him to a bend called U-Turn. He said, "For your restoration to be complete, you have to go through the U-Turn which leads back to the Pilgrims Path. It is time to go. Always remember I am within reach when you call. All you need to do is call and I will be there." Glory stepped on the bend, and with a renewed vigor, was ready to make it through. He thanked Wisdom for the rescue and said, "I will see you soon," and continued on his walk back to the Pilgrims Path. It was a tedious trip but he kept on regardless. His mind was made up. He saw a few pilgrims also making the same journey, but each one had his own route to travel through. After a while, he started hearing voices again, but this time, they were familiar voices. They sounded like the praise singers. They were chanting his name while some clapped in synchronized rhythm. As he moved closer up, the chants and claps got louder, but this time around, he could not see them. He was blind to them though he could hear them. As he continued on his walk through the U-Turn, he came to the final turn that leads back to the Pilgrims Path, and with tears in his eyes and a heart of thankfulness; he went through until he got to the path. He remembered the path and memories of his walk through this road flooded his mind. He was jolted back to reality by the murmurings and whispers around him. Strangely, he could not see those whispering but he could pick up a few words of what was being said. He realized that the same people who had been the praise singers were those who were murmuring and whispering. And the reason for their grunts was because he paid them no attention and they were shocked and surprised that this certainly could not be Glory, as the Glory they knew would acknowledge them. Many knew something had changed within him. When the murmurings and whispers stopped, Glory screamed, "I am back!" This attracted other pilgrims to him and there he shared his story of descent through the road called Detour and how Wisdom rescued him and his journey through the U-Turn bend. By the time he was done, a few pilgrims had tears in their eyes. They moved closer and hugged and kissed him. Yet, a few others were feet away from him, mocking and scorning him, but his experience had made him blind to such people. One of the pilgrims said to him, "Glory, your experience has become a lesson and example unto us. We will certainly search out what is in the pilgrim's manual as we continue in our journey and engage Wisdom at all times, but at same time, we cannot discount your valuable input in our lives." Glory responded, "The ultimate aim is to get to the Mountaintop Boulevard. Let us all travel with caution. Set our eyes on our final destination. Avoid any form of distraction and we will make it there." Glory continued on his journey to the Pilgrims Path, as did the other Pilgrims.

Chapter 6

The Last Mile

Glory kept reflecting on his recent experience and wondered why he wasn't watchful enough but was thankful for the second chance. He ensured he was completely clad in his full armor and had his shield rightly positioned as he had been reminded through his experience of the importance of the shield. As he kept walking, he realized that the numbers of pilgrims walking along the same part were reducing and the part was becoming a lonely one. Glory continued his walk until he came to the gate called, 'The Last Mile.' It was a huge gate built in such a way that it would be difficult for anyone to see what's on the other side of it. As Glory approached the gate, he remembered he had read from the manual about The Last Mile and knew immediately that this would be his final hurdle before getting to the Mountaintop. He was excited! He knelt down on the path for a moment and reflected on his journey so far with tears of joy streaming down his face. A new kind of strength surged through his being like a torrent. He stood up and continued walking until he got to the gate. He met some other pilgrims that he had recognized in the course of his journey; everyone was smiling at each other and one of the pilgrim's exclaimed, "We are almost there and we will certainly get there."

It was common knowledge for the pilgrims at the gate that they cannot go through the gate together. Every pilgrim must go through this gate on his or her own. The gate only opens to accommodate one pilgrim at a time and each one must push through the gate to get to the other side. Glory decided to take the shot. He had observed that there were pilgrims who had been at the gate for a very long time and were rather complacent about getting to see what was on the other side, but he was driven by the fact that he knew where he was heading and the gate was not his final destination. He had gone through the treasure map and he knew his treasure hunt did not end at the gate of The Last Mile. He understood that the journey had not ended. He said to himself, "I cannot come this far to rest at the gate. It is time to go through." With those words, Glory pushed on the gate and it opened up. He was greeted by a great glittering light coming from a distance. The gate shut behind him while he stood in awe of the beauty ahead of him. He knew that was the Mountaintop Boulevard. With excitement, Glory leaped for joy, exclaiming, "I can see it! I can see it!! I can see it!!!" It was a beautiful scene but the route ahead looked rough and rugged. He said to himself, "With beauty ahead of me, no route is too tough for me to get there. I have seen it. I have been through so much to get here and now I have this awesome scenery ahead, nothing will stop me even if I have to crawl on this path. I will do it," he resolved.

Glory started tracing the path of that great light with his feet but the more he walked, the farther it seemed. However, he was determined and kept on. He met some few other pilgrims on the way; some had fallen and fainted along the route. Others were holding on as it were to their last breath. Glory wanted to ignore these weary pilgrims, even though he was also tired, he was more alert than many of them. He thought to himself, "I can't leave these behind, they have come this far and are closer to the final destination than when they started." He looked into his treasure chest and reached out for the map again and it was found therein that a cistern was nearby. Glory, using the treasure map, was able to search out the cistern and collect water from there. He let a few drops go down into the mouth of the pilgrims that had fainted; they were revived and they, together with the other pilgrims, went to the cistern to scoop water to refresh their tired frames. They were thankful and everyone continued on their journey.

Glory eventually came to a small hill. Tired and worn out, he climbed to go over it. He fell in his first attempt but stood up and attempted it for the second time, but this time he went over it. Lifting up his head, he saw the foot of the Mountaintop ahead, and right on the Mountaintop, the brilliant light was so distinct. It was a beautiful array of colors. He could hear beautiful music as never heard before on the Pilgrims Path playing from the top of the Mountaintop. He was happy. "I'm almost there," he said to himself.

The Foot of the Mountaintop

He stood and kept moving. As he went through the final junction on the route, he finally came to the foot of the Mountaintop and saw many Pilgrims gathered around it. Many were chatting away. Some were just sitting on rocks that were littered around the base. He saw others who were lying on their backs and could not move. There were some others who were just content with being at the foot of the beautiful Mountain and would rather make their abode there. Glory was glad he made it to the foot of the Mountain, but his focus was the mountaintop. He lifted up his head and saw some Pilgrims climbing and making an effort to get to the Mountaintop.

Glory approached a fellow pilgrim who was sitting on one of the little rocks and who seemed not to be perturbed by all that was going on around him. "You look like someone who is satisfied with where he is," Glory said. "I have come this far and with what I have seen at the foot of the Mountaintop, I am satisfied. I have been sitting here for a very long time. Many of the pilgrims met me here. A few of them made the effort to climb to get to the Mountaintop. I have seen a few of them go through successfully and I have also seen others fall off, as they slipped and fell. That's why you have some people with their backs to the ground; they have also resigned to fate and have refused to give it another shot, although some did and went through. I don't want to go through that stress, with what I have seen at the foot of the Mountaintop, I am content. I have never felt so much relief throughout my journey. Of course, you know how assiduous the journey has been and to come, see and experience the beautiful scenery and be refreshed at the base of the Mountain is quite elating, and you know what? I am not alone. You can see the numbers for yourself. Although I can't see what is going on there at the top of the Mountain, I presume there will not be much of a difference," the pilgrim responded. "I have heard all that you have said but a look at the treasure map and the manual I have, which I believe you should have too, shows that the ultimate treasure chest is up there on the Mountaintop and I have not come this far, with all the challenges I'd faced on this journey to settle for less. My ultimate destination is to get to the Mountaintop Boulevard. I can picture Wisdom already waiting to welcome me to the beautiful Mountaintop. And I encourage you to do likewise," Glory concluded.

Step by Step - Grip by Grip

Glory turned and faced the Mountain and with his face set as a flint, he took the first step on his final climb to the Mountaintop Boulevard. He was resolved in his heart to get to the Mountaintop regardless of whatever betides. One step at a time, he went up the mountain. Grip by grip, he pulled himself up. "I wish I could run up the mountain. Is there something I could do better to make my climb easier?" He was not deterred. "If there are pilgrims who made it through to the Mountaintop and went through this same route, I certainly can do the same," he said. He was not alone; other pilgrims were climbing and everyone was focused on getting to the top. Glory approached a cleft by the side of the mountain and there he saw some pilgrims scooping with their hands water that flowed from the cleft. He decided to do the same as he was already weary from his journey. He saw some familiar faces there; a few of which he had never exchanged any words with while on the Pilgrims Path. Quite a number were also not known. He could not remember anyone making reference to anyone of these while they were on the Pilgrims Path. These were the quiet ones who faithfully travelled the Pilgrims Path. It was an opportunity to meet these pilgrims and engage them before getting to the Mountaintop Boulevard. Glory approached one of them, "I have seen your face a few times on the Pilgrims Path although we did not interact." Glory said, wanting to start a conversation. "I know you well. You were one of the popular pilgrims and a blessing to many. You did a wonderful job out there and helped make some of the pilgrim's burdens lighter," the other pilgrim responded. Glory answered, "I have no regret that I did all that. The problem was that I allowed it to get into me. I almost lost it. I learnt a huge lesson from the whole experience and it made me better prepared for the rest of my journey. The most important thing is that I am here now; a few steps to the Mountaintop Boulevard." "I was able to touch the lives of a few pilgrims too, but what I avoided was the spotlight. I had a choice to travel through the Highland of Fame but I ignored it and continued my journey on the rough Pilgrims Path. I discovered early on that I might not be able to survive a walk through that land. I have heard of pilgrims who went through the Highland of Fame and they were able to survive it, and they are on this mountain climbing journey with us. Whether you went through the Highland of Fame or not and whether you had challenges that almost crippled your journey or not, what is important is that we are here, a few steps away from our final destination. We need to maintain focus because it is not over yet until we arrive on the mountaintop," he said. They hugged each other and after a few more scoops of water to quench his thirst, Glory continued on his climb to the Mountaintop. Now, he could hear the beautiful music from the mountaintop. There was something about the music being played as it came with a refreshing air that gave succor and comfort to the pilgrims. As the music played, he heard voices singing with one of the most beautiful melodies he had ever heard, and they sang the following words:

"Well done thou weary pilgrim

Thy King awaits thee

You have not come this far

To eventually let go

On your grip.

A few more steps

And you will be home

Hold on firmly

For Your King Awaits thee."

That song was like a booster shot. Glory renewed his resolve that he would make it to the Mountaintop no matter the situation. As if to test his resolve, suddenly, there was a strong wind advancing towards them. Glory held tenaciously with a grip as he whispered, "I will not let go. I will make it to the boulevard." The wind encircled around the pilgrims and was quite ferocious, and no pilgrim could take another step because of the strong impact. When it calmed, Glory was still holding on tight. With a look to his left and right sides, he observed that some pilgrims could not survive the wind; they were blown off. His heart was heavy. He remembered the words of the pilgrim he spoke to in the cleft: "It is not over until you get to the Mountaintop." "How true this is," he thought. One step, one grip, Glory continued until he looked up and saw he was just steps away from the cliff of the Mountaintop Boulevard.

I Made It

Glory held onto the cliff of the Mountaintop. A hand touched him. He looked up and found one of the most glorious and awesome Beings. The appearance was sparkling. The Being stooped low and pulled Glory up. With tears of joy streaming down the eyes of Glory, he said, "I made it!" He kept repeating that as he leaped for joy, not minding who it was that pulled him up. It was an exhilarating moment. After a while, he regained his composure and looked curiously at the one standing right before him after a prolonged stare, he screamed, "Wisdom! You are Wisdom!" Wisdom nodded with a smile. Glory walked close and hugged Wisdom, and with tears streaming down his eyes again, he whispered,

"Thank you! Thank you!! Thank you!!!" as he held closely unto Him. Wisdom responded, "I'm glad you made it. You are welcome. It has been a pretty long journey from Valleytown and now for the final time, I will have to take you by the hand through the Victor's Gate.

Chapter 7

The Mountaintop Boulevard#

Hand in hand, Wisdom and Glory walked from the Precipice of the Mountaintop towards the Victor's Gate which led into the very expansive Mountaintop Boulevard. "We will need to take off your armor, as it is no longer needed here. As soon as we go through the Victor's Gate, you will be brought into the Corridor of Mercy that opens up to the Boulevard. There is an awesome transformation that will take place while you walk through this corridor. Your battered armor will drop off you and be replaced by the most beautifully crafted apparel anyone has ever seen. This was made by the Prince Charming Himself. Everyone that has gone through the tough and rugged Pilgrims Path deserves the very best when they arrive at the Mountaintop. You have fought a good fight. You stayed on track and regardless of the few challenges on the journey, you are one of the finest and you deserve the warmest welcome," Wisdom said.

The Sight and Scene

The gate opened of its own accord as they moved close. There were beautifully cladded guards on both sides of the gate waving and cheering Glory as he walked past the Victor's Gate into the Corridor of Mercy and on the wall was written, "Taking your mess and giving you His mercy." Glory could not express his joy. He was in a state of ecstasy and absolute peace. As he walked through the Mercy corridor, his old and scarred armor fell off and was immediately replaced by a pure glowing silverine trim-fitted apparel just as mentioned by Wisdom. "The mountaintop Boulevard must have class," he thought. While he was trying to figure out the transformation that was taking place, he observed that his skin had changed also. There was no more hair on his body and all the scars were gone. A skin regeneration had occurred. He could see all that was going on in high definition through the reflection on the wall of the corridor. There was a transparent and glistening curtain at the end of the corridor of Mercy and as Glory walked towards the exit, there were shower drops coming from the sprinklers above, which left no wetness but rather a gentle and sweet fragrance that had never been perceived before. At the exit above was written, "Welcome Chosen." As Glory walked through the transparent curtain, he was in awe of what he saw. There was a Guard of Honor singing and playing on diverse kinds of instruments as he exited the Mercy corridor. It was a beautiful sight to behold. Nothing could be compared to the splendor and ambience of this land. Everything exudes purity, class and unrivaled glitz. The Guards of Honor followed Glory behind as the leader of the guard led him towards the huge and brightly lit Colosseum at the center of the Boulevard. It was a huge jamboree. He turned to Glory and said, "You are welcome. You have done well and you deserve the heroic welcome you have received. We do this for every Chosen that comes through the Corridor of Mercy. You will notice that I mentioned Chosen and not Pilgrim. On the Mountaintop, we do not have pilgrims here. As soon as you come through the Corridors of Mercy you leave your past behind. Everyone who has travelled through the Pilgrims Path and made it through the Victor's Gate is called the Redeemed. You have done well," concluded the leader of the Guard. While Glory was still trying to soak in the reality of what was happening, he heard his name called from the side. He turned and saw Mentor beckoning to him from the side. "I am glad you made it. When I got here, I asked if you had arrived but was told you were still on your way," he said. Glory ran towards him and embraced him. "I almost missed it if not for Mercy and Wisdom," Glory uttered. "Many did miss it but I am happy we both made it. The battles are over. We are now the Chosen," Mentor responded. As they approached the huge and beautifully built Colosseum, Glory could not contain his joy. He had never seen anything like it. The Colosseum was a beauty to behold; a masterpiece of superlative architectural expertise. A beautiful blend of colors emanating from the center of the Colosseum gave the most beautiful display of light anyone could ever see. As they walked through the entrance of the Colosseum, there was a thunderous applause and voices that seemed to respond in perfect symphony sang:

"You are here,

You fought and conquered

Now into His endless joy

and splendor You will abide

No more battle! No more toils!!

Welcome thou Chosen."

All the chosen already seated in the Colosseum stood up while still clapping their hands for those just arriving. It was an electrifying moment. The sight of everyone clad in the silverine trim-fitted apparel was beyond description. There was not a single moment of dullness. The atmosphere was ecstatic. The serenity of the environment was peaceful. As the music faded, Wisdom, who was now in front, said, "Oh King! Full of splendor and honor, I present to you the new entrants who have come from afar, fought and overcame and held firmly thereto without wavering. They are the Chosen." The King of the Mountaintop Boulevard was indescribable. There is no word in the vocabulary of anyone that can qualify and quantify Him. The regality, the splendor and honor he exudes cannot be explained. His eyes are like fireballs which turn in circles and His love and compassion cannot be compared. The same goes for the Prince Charming; whenever he smiles, it's like a gentle breeze that flows through the Mountaintop.

The Prince Charming stood on his feet and all the congregation of the Chosen in unity bowed their heads. He walked down the stairs from where he was with a glittering crown on His head. Wisdom stepped to the side and beckoned for the newly arrived Chosen to walk towards the Prince Charming. For every Chosen that arrived, the Prince Charming gave the warmest embrace and instructed that they be taken to the seat prepared for them in the Colosseum and thereafter shown where the treasures they have sought are found.

With an air of fulfillment, Glory sat on the seat reserved for him. He was informed that at the end of the induction, he would be taken to his place of abode specially prepared for him and shown his treasures. "You have never seen anything like it," said the guard who escorted him to his seat.

On A Final Note

It's been a journey working on this project which has been divinely inspired by God Himself. It's taken over 18 months to work particularly on this book. I may not be able to pen God's dealings during this period because they are very deep. Sometimes, I am awoken in the very early hours of the day and inspired to continue writing and after a certain period, the inspiration will cease. And many times, I have gone through what has been written and could not figure out if these words came from my pen, as they truly did not.

I strongly encourage you to read through this timeless work with an open mind. Let the Lord Himself minister to you. There are deep truths embedded on these pages and their applications will help our journey as we travel along.

I will leave you with this final note: whatever you do, make sure you do it with heaven in view. Also, know it is God's will for you to make it through the tough challenges of life and succeed. There will certainly be oppositions as we pursue our goals here on earth and as we continue in our journey to heaven, but whatever happens, don't lose your focus. Be determined like Glory that 'come what may,' you will never give up. You will continue to run the race and focus on Jesus, who is the Author and the Finisher of our Faith.

Contact Details:

Email: **gmattoki@gmail.com**

gbenga@gbengaowotoki.com

Website: **http://gbengaowotoki.com**

Facebook: **www.facebook.com/gbenga.owotoki**

Twitter: **@GbengaOwotoki**

Made in the USA
Columbia, SC
25 May 2017